About the Author

NEIL BIERBAUM (B.Com) has been a life and executive coach since 2005 and has practised and taught meditation for more than 25 years. He has worked with large corporates, SMEs, entrepreneurs and private clients—many of them looking to manage the enormous stress and increasing complexity in their professional and personal lives and make sure they achieve their potential in an uncertain world.

www.neilbierbaum.com

Personal Effectiveness

Also by Neil Bierbaum

BOOKS

Practical Mindfulness

A handbook for self-development, combining the best of mindfulness, coaching and CBT. Co-authored by clinical psychologist and cognitive behaviour therapy (CBT) specialist Dr Colinda Linde.

The Conscious Leader: 52 Leadership Maxims

Weekly readings to guide your leadership reflections.

The Personal Effectiveness Series

Personal Effectiveness

Personal Effectiveness for Executives

The Personal Effectiveness Self-Coaching Handbook

The Personal Effectiveness Self-Coaching Handbook for Executives

ONLINE COURSES

Self-Coaching Online | Life

An online version of the Personal Effectiveness Life Coaching Program.

Self-Coaching Online | Executive

An online version of the Personal Effectiveness Executive Coaching Program.

Practical Mindfulness

An online version of this six-module applied mindfulness program.

WEBSITES

www.neilbierbaum.com

www.themanmatrix.com

www.practicalmindfulness.co.za

Personal Effectiveness

12 coaching tools to increase your leverage over life's challenges and win more often!

NEIL BIERBAUM

Alembic

Published by ALEMBIC (Pty) Ltd

1 Disa, 55 Witney St, Bryanston, 2191

Gauteng, South Africa

info@alembic.co.za

First Edition

Paperback ISBN: 978-0-6398237-0-6

e-Book ISBN: 978-0-6398237-1-3

Visit the author's website at

www.neilbierbaum.com

Contents

Preface 11

About Coaching 13

About Personal Effectiveness 29

1 | Getting Motivated 31

2 | Know Yourself 43

3 | Working with Values 55

4 | Your Power to Create 65

5 | Decision & Commitment 77

6 | Story & Reality 87

7 | Taking Responsibility 95

8 | Working with Emotions 107

9 | The Red Zone 119

10 | The State of Flow 133

11 | The Habit of Completion 145

12 | Legacy & Lifestyle 155

Epilogue | True Leadership 179

BIBLIOGRAPHY 181

FURTHER RESOURCES 184

for Colinda, thank you for getting me

for Luke, thank you for believing in me

Acknowledgements

In the personal and leadership development field, a lot of information gets shared, adapted, reused and repurposed, especially in workshop settings, to the extent that it's not always possible to accurately determine the originator of an idea, representation or piece of work.

As far as possible, and to the best of my knowledge, I have credited people for their work, using standard publishing conventions, when I know that they've originated it themselves and/or that they've published the work in their name. I have not credited the source for information I've gleaned by attending a paid course, workshop, coach training or professional development program, in cases where I'm confident that they were not the originator or copyright holder for the information being presented.

I acknowledge Marc Steinberg, founder of the Consciousness Coaching Academy, as being the first person from whom I heard the following broad concepts: your power to create using words; story and reality; commitment; completion; authenticity. I have credited Marc directly for the *Ladder of Power*, which is his original creation. I acknowledge Colin Adam of Ennea International as being the person from whom I first learned about the enneagram and the *Four Conversations* model, which I have adapted into the *Five-Phase Conversation Model*. I acknowledge Dr John Demartini as being the person from whom I first heard about people's commitment to their values and the ordering and prioritising of values. I acknowledge Dr Colinda Linde, from whom I learned about dealing with emotions using the cognitive behaviour therapy (CBT) method defined in David Barlow's *Unified Protocol*.

I believe I have adapted all of the above concepts and advanced their representation sufficiently to claim copyright on this particular formulation of the information. I do claim to be the originator of the following concepts and models: the organisation of motivational states into five levels and naming them, except the flow state); the *Red Zone* concept and solution model; the three levels of honesty.

My Personal Mission

My commitment is to make a real, tangible difference in the world, to the way people conduct their lives. To inspire, touch and move people to grow consciously, which means to gain greater self-awareness and thereby improve self-management in order to have a different, better experience of life; and to act for the greatest good (harmony and ongoing, shared prosperity) of all spheres of life.

My Promise to Deliver

I promise to deliver a state of optimal performance through mindful awareness and personal mastery, a result which I call *Personal Effectiveness*. Personal Effectiveness means having the personal power to consciously achieve optimal performance in service of your most meaningful goals while remaining present and peaceful in the midst of life's turbulence.

People high in personal effectiveness experience being *authentic & successful, confident, caring & conscious,* and *powerful & peaceful.*

Preface

THE JOURNEY to write this book began some thirty-odd years ago, when I told my father, after a year of articles, that I did not want to become an accountant, but a writer. There was no such thing as coaching back then, and so I didn't really have a strategy or a plan. All I knew was I had a burning hunger to understand life and to write about it. One thing I did do was to take a literary tour of America, reading all the great writers—Hemingway, Faulkner, Miller, Steinbeck, Kerouac, Bellow—in the places where they'd either written or set their most notable works.

It took a few spectacular coincidences—or blessings from above—for me to find a steady path and enjoy a successful career as a journalist and, ultimately, a magazine editor. Still, it was not enough. I wanted to go deeper.

During that time, a magazine crossed my desk with a feature on men who called themselves coaches and did this thing of sharing wisdom with others. I'd been exposed to motivational speakers for many years and had found them fundamentally fake. I had never thought to do that, but when I saw the possibility for gaining and sharing wisdom, I was on board.

Coaching wasn't really a "thing" back then and it took me a few more years to find a coach training school—and the right one for me, one that promised wisdom and insight, and not just "success in business". I trained and have practised as a coach for fifteen years now. I also trained as a trainer and trained other people to become coaches and coach trainers. They say you only really learn something when you teach it and I can attest to that.

One thing I know for sure, is that as lost as I was in the beginning, I really found something in coaching. It has given me the understanding that I was after. And I'm not talking about flaky beliefs here. I'm a great sceptic and not easily convinced. I drove my father mad as a child with my questioning, and during my coach training I became a major irritation to the trainers for the same reason. I always need to go to the source, or the foundation, to be sure. Eventually, I became convinced that the approach I learned was the real deal. I learned to see things as they are, without delusion, and to work only in ways that really make a difference.

One more thing I know for sure is that if I'd had coaching, especially during those early years, it would have made a massive difference to my progress through life and career. I've seen that be the case for my clients and I've often thought how fortunate we are—especially the young among us—to live in a time when we can be exposed to this modality.

Every day of my journey as a coach, everything I've seen and learned, I've treated as research. I've added it to the pile of knowledge and wisdom that I've gained—not only through practising coaching, but also living it, trying it, testing it and seeing what works to improve your personal effectiveness. I'll unpack that term properly later on this book, but for now you can take it to mean successfully managing yourself through the vicissitudes of life, in all areas of life. Knowing what's going on and knowing that you know what you're doing. Being able to manage yourself in any situation. Being the best person you can be, both in life and in business.

Every day, I've wanted to take that knowledge and wisdom and share it by writing—one form of which would be an effective self-help book, one that I would have wanted to read, one that would have made a difference for me. I've held the belief that if I approach it in this way, it will be effective for others. So, after many years and many attempts, this is my offering.

This book brings together all the essential elements of a foundational coaching program. It can be read on its own and serves as a valuable accompaniment to my live and online coaching programs. In this book you'll find slightly more detail than the notes offered via the online program, while the online program has video and audio options designed to suit different learning styles.

Neil Bierbaum
Johannesburg, South Africa
July 2019

About Coaching

EVERY ONE of us has a dream, a goal, a passion, a lifestyle that we want to pursue. Set against that we have beliefs that limit us. You might want to start your own business, but believe deep down that you don't have the skills, or can't afford the risk. Getting fit, getting educated, finding the right relationship partner. In all of these areas there is something that you would most likely have if you could and you were honest with yourself. Weighing heavily on anyone is the belief that it's too late, that you're not good enough, that life doesn't work like that, and so on. Coaching supports you to recognise these two conversations as they exist inside you and to make empowered choices about which one to live your life by.

Modern society presents people with unprecedented challenges and opportunities. There is the opportunity to create your own path and fulfil your destiny. The flipside of this coin is the challenge to define yourself without the strong social reference points of religion, job, social class that past generations relied upon.

There is the opportunity that technology presents for personal marketing, communication and commercial leverage. With this comes the challenge of managing your time and staying abreast of the latest developments.

There is a wide range of new opportunities for education and wealth creation. This presents the challenge of managing the rate of change by which knowledge and wealth creation strategies become obsolete as quickly as they are learned.

Self-management and life management are needed in a way that they were not needed before, and coaching steps into this space. Coaching is a means by which you can become self-sufficient in a world where self-sufficiency has taken on a whole new meaning.

The principles and practices of self-sufficiency that coaching delivers are relevant to all areas of life, including the corporate work space, the small, privately-owned business space and in people's personal lives.

About life coaching

What if everybody really, honestly, does have a unique gift, something that they can do better than anybody else in the world? Wouldn't you want to know what yours is? And if you identified it, wouldn't you want to develop that gift and express it?

Most often, when we think about a person's gift, or "genius", we think of the obvious ones, like being a great artist, musician, sportsperson or actor. Then we decide, well, I don't have any of those, and we put our head down and get on with life. Yet, what if your gift is something more subtle, like devising spreadsheet models, trading antiques or icing cakes? Or even less tangible, like being an expert communicator, negotiator, or nurturer of people? And being able to do that thing better than anyone else you know, perhaps better than anyone else in the world?

Some people discover their gift early and life supports them to express it, perhaps even to earn their living from it. Others know what it is, but life doesn't support them to express it early on—parents don't recognise it, teachers reject it as useless, or it simply gets crowded out by adverse conditions. Still others don't even recognise the possibility that there could be anything special about themselves, until one day they grow tired of just going through the motions and finally ask the question, "What if...?"

What if you could discover your own unique gifts and find a way to express them in the world? If you're knocking on that door, then that would be a good reason to engage in a life coaching program. It's designed expressly for that purpose.

Life coaching is goal-directed and effective

Then there's another "What if...?" that you can ask. It goes like this: What if success means being the best version of yourself that you can be? This means, apart from finding and expressing your unique gift, just being a great human being, improving yourself on all fronts, for no other reason than that—being the best version of yourself that you can be. We'd call this personal mastery, to use a term coined by the modern leadership guru Peter Senge, who described it as people's ability to learn about themselves and apply that learning to their choices and behaviours in order to be more effective in every context. Or we could use Aristotle's term, *eudaimonia*, which can be loosely interpreted to mean a process of self-improvement through conscious effort, as a result of which you will flourish in all areas of life. If it's that you're after, then, once again, life coaching is one of the most effective vehicles you can choose.

Of course, for some people, it's not even about that. Twenty-first century life is so complex and challenging that, sometimes, it's enough just to get on top of things—and stay on top. If you could just improve your relationships or make better relationship choices. For some, that would be a great outcome and make a massive difference to their lives. For others, it could be to improve decision-making. Or to handle your emotions better, or just behave better in general. Perhaps to gain discipline in order to exercise or eat better. Or to find a purpose early in life, or to reignite a sense of purpose later in life. Many people turn to therapy for these things, and often that turns into an endless search for causes in childhood and family dynamics. While that can lead to a useful understanding of influencers, it can also be limited in terms of changing your productive outputs.

So, if you're looking to make significant behavioural changes, or get on top of your personal performance and effectiveness, then life coaching can be a much more goal-directed and effective path than long-term therapy.

So then, what do you want your life to be about? More to the point, what are you waiting for?

What is a life coaching program?

Life coaching is not psychoanalysis and it's not—or shouldn't be—a bunch of airy-fairy New Age mumbo jumbo or positive thinking. You don't have to delve into your past, or say how you felt about this or that experience when you were a child. You don't have to bare your soul. You don't even have to share all the details of what you're working through.

Your coach will support you to work out your desired outcomes, and agree the number of sessions, so that there's a definite beginning, middle and end to the process. The sessions are typically 45-60 minutes duration and can be conducted in person or by telephone / videocall. Sessions are normally held weekly or fortnightly.

During each session, you'll face down a set of strong, clear questions that should give you the clarity to see what's standing in your way, and what you need to do. The questions are designed to give you instant clarity, focus and purpose. It's like calling in a lawnmower or interior design specialist. You'll wonder why you ever struggled for so long with that issue.

The questioning process that is typical of coaching as a modality is joined by a process of awareness creation (how life really works and how, by applying certain principles and practices, you can make it work for you) and of accountability (checking that you follow through and do what you decide).

Outcomes you can expect from a life coaching program:

- Being able to recognize and change disempowering internal beliefs;
- The awareness to instantly recognise and redirect negative thoughts, moods, emotions;
- The strength to change destructive and unwanted habits;
- The ability to accurately observe and gain insights into yourself (without unnecessary self-analysis);
- A sense of knowing who you are, what you deserve, and how you can, and will, get there;
- The power to express yourself in the world and demonstrate the results that you feel you deserve.

What this can do for your life:

- Improved moods and energy;
- Clarity of purpose and decisiveness;
- Being firm, and being flexible;
- Confidence in the future;
- Inspiring and influencing others;
- Improved relationships;
- Getting off your butt and not procrastinating;
- Actually achieving goals that you set yourself;
- A broader view of how the world works;
- A general sense of well-being and happiness.

Climbing the inner mountain

Many people who approach coaching feel that they need to have some heroic goal, like climbing Kilimanjaro, for example. Such acts are noble, and accomplishing them will give anyone a strong sense of satisfaction and pride. In particular, you'll feel that you've conquered your own limitations created by fear and doubt.

Then you'll return to your day-to-day life and, chances are, not much will change. Mostly, the answers you'll come up with will be the same ones, only you'll be more determined and courageous than before. This might, however, lead to you doing whatever it was you were doing, just harder, faster, louder, with more courage and determination. You risk repeating the same mistakes, but worse.

The coaching process confronts you with your inner mountain. It gets you to catch yourself in the act of creating your own life—to see your cognitive mistakes, your ineffective practices, and so on. It can be just as challenging as climbing a real mountain in terms of pushing you to find that inner strength, determination and courage. In addition, because you're doing it on the field of play, in your daily life, you really get to learn the lesson and then apply the lesson. This leads to real change, real transformation where it matters most—in your real life, not on some distant mountain.

If you can handle the process, you'll come away a more effective person with a deeper appreciation of yourself, your life and others.

But will it help me?

Life coaching can be relevant for many more "issues" than most people realise. Of course, it's purpose-built for helping you find your purpose, improve your mindset, develop self-discipline and self-mastery, perform at your best and achieve your goals. The list below will give a sense of some additional issues that people seek to address, and which coaching can make a difference on—if you have the right coach.

Anxiety & worry

Anxiety is a common problem that people seek help for. Sometimes, it can be debilitating, in which case you should seek out a diagnosis from a clinical psychologist or psychiatrist, and follow the prescribed treatment.

As soon as you can, however, and certainly if you're not suffering from a clinical level of anxiety, you would do well to look into life coaching as a modality for helping you to deal with your anxiety.

The key symptom or indicator of anxiety is being overly focused on possible negative futures, and being overly convinced that they will actually happen. One of the outcomes of effective life coaching is to bring you into the present, and to train you to deal with what's real and what you can influence, rather than what's imagined.

Life coaching can support you to learn a method of self-management that includes setting goals and taking action to achieve them. This will enable you to develop the habit of becoming task-focused, which keeps you out of those bad neighbourhoods of negative thinking.

Depression

Depression has become increasingly common in recent times. Statistics show that as much as 25% of the workforce in some countries is being treated for depression. Mental health awareness has led to government budgets in some of those countries being dedicated to treating this phenomenon.

As with anxiety, depression can be debilitating. And similarly, when that's the case, you should seek out a diagnosis from a clinical psychologist or psychiatrist, and follow the recommended or prescribed treatment.

However, the way out of depression is not to sit for months or years unpacking your feelings or your childhood. Just as anxiety is future based, the key symptom or indicator of depression is ruminating about the past: lamenting a deprived childhood; beating yourself up for things you did or didn't do, or bad decisions you made; wishing things could have happened or turned out differently. So, to the extent that traditional psychotherapy tends to focus on past events and feelings and their possible causes, it's not always the best way to shift you out of a state of depression.

One of the outcomes of effective life coaching is to get you to focus on future goals that excite and inspire you; to bring you into the present; and to train you to deal with what's real and what you can influence, rather than what's in the past. In addition, life coaching is particularly effective with what's called "behavioural activation". That means getting you to actually try on new behaviours and establish those as good habits—and that's an important, *proven* element in the recovery from depression.

Life coaching will also show you that you can "let go" of the past without having to analyse it to death—that closure can be achieved by virtue of a decision and does not require an exhaustive rehashing of the event.

You might also want to look at the context in which your depression is occurring. If it's timed to coincide with a life-stage crisis (midlife or the more recently defined quarter-life crisis), for example, and especially if a major symptom is a lack of purpose or meaning or direction, then you can count life coaching as a modality that might help you to deal with that.

In all of the above, you can see that life coaching can support you to learn a method of self-management that includes setting goals and taking action to achieve them. This means you can learn to develop a stable and replicable—and therefore sustainable and independent—pathway out of depression.

Stress & burnout

Stress is what you experience when the demands placed on you are outweighed by the available resources. In the corporate and business world today, there is an ongoing drive to do more with less—less money and less time. Technology was supposed to be a resource, to help us, yet in many cases it's become a channel for additional demands instead.

Burnout is the consequence of relentless, ongoing stress. In many cases it can look and feel like depression, however there is a key distinction: depression is more pervasive—you feel unilaterally flat and don't care about anything; burnout is more specifically work-related—you'll still feel better on a Friday when there's no work, but you'll feel like giving up as you approach Monday, and having to go back to work.

Your ability to handle stress and avert—or recover from—burnout can be addressed through a multi-pronged approach: improving your ability to mentally reframe things and think differently (changing your relationship to the situation); getting clear on your values and what really matters to you, then being able to set boundaries and say no; developing your ability to—and belief that you can—solve your own problems; and having a sense that life—whether in the form of God, of other people, or simply coincidence and flow—can and does support you.

These are precisely what life coaching, using an outcomes-oriented approach, is designed to teach, train and instil.

Life-stage crises

The shift from one life stage to another is often dramatic and experienced as some form of crisis. The first one happens right when we're born. OK, life coaching can't help you there. But then there's puberty, in which case you'll probably need a specialist teenage life coach. Then comes young adulthood, which includes the big choices around getting married (or not) and parenting (or not), as well as making the first big moves in your chosen career.

Nowadays there's the quarter-life crisis and we all know about the midlife crisis. Given that we're finding ourselves more healthy in old age, there's another steam train on its way: the "rewire instead of retire" crisis, or what to do in your mature years.

In each of these instances, you're letting go of old reference points, and latching onto, or defining, new ones. There's always confusion as you discover that old tricks no longer work, and you have to figure out new ones. There can also be regret or shame when you find that old defences are no longer needed. For example, you might find yourself thinking, *Why was I so angry all the time?*

The trick with a life-phase crisis is to recognise it as such, and learn to surf it like the wave that it is, instead of getting tumbled by it. Use it as a chance to ask some really good questions, re-evaluate, define new goals, develop a new strategy, perhaps a whole new way of being, and make some solid plans that you can take action on.

When you accept that each life-stage crisis is actually a necessary and inevitable transition, you can approach it consciously, and navigate it with awareness and intent. Life coaching is built for this purpose. By engaging in a program, you can emerge from each life-stage transition with greater wisdom and personal power, and set a meaningful course for the next stage.

Relationship strife

One of the challenges people often have when they visit a couples counsellor is that the counsellor drives too hard towards an assumed outcome—the couple making peace, or staying together. This usually ends up with one person (the dragger) who feels that their agenda is being heard, while the other one (the dragee) feeling distinctly unheard and under pressure.

An essential element of good life coaching is finding out from the client what they want—and if there's two of them, to first establish and agree what they both want. The coach has no agenda and is not afraid of where things might go. Therefore, both people feel heard. This alone makes a massive difference to the process. (It's important to note that this is a developed competence on the part of the coach—just think about how much people are inclined to offer their opinion and give advice; coaches are specifically trained to NOT do that.)

In addition, a core element of life coaching is to develop an awareness in the client of the power of language and how to use it more effectively. That means, firstly, developing better self-talk and, secondly, improving your ability to communicate with others, including how you send out communication (what you say and how you say it) and how you receive it (how you listen and what you listen for). Naturally, better self-talk leads to better personal performance and improved communication skills leads to improved relationships.

In fact, a large part of *executive* coaching is applying everything that's described above in the workplace context. Similarly, life coaching can be equally effective in achieving the same outcomes for people's personal and intimate relationships.

Coaching for men

Men are going to get a special mention here. The reason is that women tend to have better support networks. They share, they attend courses, they more readily seek help. If you run a public weekend workshop for women, you'll easily get a hundred or more signing up! If you try to stage a public weekend workshop for men, on the other hand, you'll be lucky to get five. Unless it's linked to a church, then that's a different story—you'll get thousands.

The bottom line is that most men who face challenges think they're the only ones. Therefore, they think that if they go to a workshop, they'll make a fool of themselves in front of other men. The truth is, when they do attend, they very quickly realise that they're not alone. This makes it OK to share, and suddenly they find themselves being supported by other men. That's usually a strange experience for most men.

Men also think that they should be able to face things alone. They look around at their friends' apparently perfect lives and ask themselves, What's wrong with me? Then they'll retreat into the respective workshop of their own minds, and try to fix it all themselves.

In the old days, men did that. They fixed their own cars, too. There was no coaching for men back then, just as there were no cell phones, or computers. These days, cars are just too hi-tech, so you take it to a specialist; you earn what's needed and you pay for the service. The same applies to your life. There are so many more moving parts in this day and age, and the old reference points of old boys' club, social norms and religion no longer suffice. Being a husband, a lover, a father, a boss, a work colleague, and staying fit and healthy in a world of abundant temptations, just isn't what it used to be. The old lonesome cowboy approach just doesn't work anymore.

So, coaching works for men and it's OK you find yourself here. The bottom line is, you can be silent (as in try to work it all out in your head) or you can be successful in all areas of your life. It's up to you.

Which life phase are you in?

Coaching is relevant for all men in all phases of life. The list below will give a sense of the typical issues that men seek to address during each phase, and which coaching can make a difference on.

Young men entering adulthood (18-25)

For young men recently out of school, studying, or otherwise making important life choices, the world can be a confusing place. There is a host of contradictory messages and things happen at an unprecedented pace.

At the same time, liberal, modern upbringings often fail to deliver the old-fashioned elements of manhood. Yes, those things like self-discipline, focus, accountability, honour and integrity. Nevertheless, life still demands these, even from boys who can cry.

Coaching can support you to learn a method of self-management, otherwise known as discipline. It can help you to recognize and develop your strengths. It can show you how to leverage those in a future that will look very different. It can also help you to recognise and manage your own reactive triggers—those things we all do when we're at our worst and which eventually lead us into trouble.

Through all of the above, it can help you to anticipate the unseen pitfalls that an over-reliance on youthful optimism may bring about.

Young adult men (ages 26-35)

For young, adult men embarking on a serious career path, marriage and/or fatherhood, there is often the question of how to take on commitments without losing yourself.

Those who ask this question now, and deal with it effectively through a coaching program, are more likely to develop a strong and stable sense of self and less likely to wake up in crisis at 40.

The pressures mount quickly during this phase. In addition to the above, developing an effective coping style and learning the art of relating to others (spouse, children, colleagues, friends) is a survival-level requirement.

Some young men seek to go one step further: they want to develop a life philosophy and learn to inspire others to follow it. A life coaching, and in particular an executive coaching, program will support you to achieve that.

Men in midlife (36-45)

If we are honest, most men only begin to have an idea of what's going on at this stage of life. Some make the mistake of trying to do it all again, but bigger, better, faster, harder. Others retreat stoically and risk the slide into despair. Neither approach is appropriate if one wants to end the game with some mix of achievement, fulfilment, wisdom and joy.

The question most men have at this stage is how to have another go at life, taking into account all one has learned, and as far as possible without doing harm. What many fail to understand or accept is that the answers are never black and white. In addition, the force and drive that they rode to distant horizons in the first half of the journey are not the vehicles for the way back.

There has been a lot said about the midlife crisis, and people are quick to make fun of it. Yet it's a necessary and inevitable phase. Approached with conscious intent, it can be managed with dignity. A man can emerge from it with greater wisdom and personal power.

Coaching can help you to understand that the task of the second half of life involves coming to terms with perceived failures. It's about letting go of the impact of wrong decisions and missed opportunities that will never come back. It's about allowing the truth of yourself to come out. Then it's about integrating the lessons and setting a meaningful course for the power years that lie ahead.

Men in the power years (46-55)

Men have received a lot of bad press lately, and it's often directed at, or felt most acutely by, the men in this phase: the power years. Most have kept their head down, worked hard and done what they were told, and find themselves exactly where they ought to be. Yet they carry the blame for thousands of years of history.

What nobody except them seems to know is just how much they've had to sacrifice of themselves in order to do what was expected, even demanded, of them.

Then there are those who feel that, despite equally keeping their heads down and staying at it, they have missed out. Fortunately, in this era, longevity gives us greater hope for another round. As the saying goes, "fifty is the new thirty".

The main issue that many men seek to deal with during this phase is making sure that at least the most meaningful life goals are achieved. Beyond achieving those goals, many men seek to define and create a legacy. Some want to establish a vision for "giving back".

Life coaching can support you to integrate all the lessons you've learned and apply that towards attaining these goals.

Mature men (56+)

Men are made to work. While many men aim to "retire by 40", that usually doesn't mean they want to stop working or doing stuff. Instead, it means they want to put money to work rather than work for money.

Then there are those men who would rather die than retire and stay home. And some do—die, that is: soon after they are forced into retirement.

The notion of retirement was established in order to create jobs for young men entering the work force during the Industrial Age. In the Information Age, and given the increase in life expectancy and vitality into old age, retiring has become "rewiring".

In many cases this simply means older men who seek to leverage the value of their experience. Many have not planned adequately for their retirement and need to do this out of necessity. For those who have, this represents the chance to do something that they were not able to do when climbing the corporate ladder and supporting a family. Then there are those who are all about finding ways to give back, whether by setting up charity foundations or investment funds, or mentoring others.

Either way, life coaching can help you create a meaningful journey for this phase of life.

The tools I use

Many people perceive coaching training to be a "weekend course" and so believe that there can't be much skill involved, and that anyone can do it. That may be true in some instances. As with any professional training, you'll get schools of different quality, and people with different levels of fit to the profession and different levels of commitment.

I'll confidently say that I've invested as much in my coaching training, in terms of money, time, blood, sweat and tears, as people do in a clinical psychology master's program, or an MBA. There are many coaches I know who could say the same. Coaching is now available through most universities and business schools and so you can get an actual master's degree in coaching. However, an academic qualification is not necessarily the key to being a great coach.

To be a great coach you have to understand, not only life, work and people, but also, and in particular, how to *cause transformation*. In fact, it goes beyond understanding. You can read a book to understand a bicycle, but you need the competence of balance if you're going to ride the bicycle. This doesn't mean the coach has to be a champion cyclist. The coach has to get someone who doesn't know they want to ride and who, when they discover the possibility, are either disdainful or afraid, and get them to ride in such a way that they feel inspired to become a great cyclist. Whether they continue that journey or not is up to them. To do this, a coach needs to have gone through their own, similar, transformation, though not necessarily with the same content.

So, if you want to find out if your coach is for real, ask to hear about their own transformation journey. They should be able to tell you who they were and who they became, and how they got there. They should be able to tell you what they learned about life and people that enables them to make a difference—and what that difference is that they can make. Then they can tell you about the tools they use. Then, if you're really interested, you can ask about their qualifications.

My personal transformation journey will be told in a separate book, although you'll find some bits and pieces in the real-life examples provided in this one. For now, I will say this: my major transformation was to go from being someone who was overloaded with ideas and analysis to someone who can see things simply and clearly; from convoluted to simple, direct communication; from being serious and clumsy when trying to make a joke to being able to get a whole room to laugh; from finding it difficult to shift my moods, to being able to shift them instantly by decision. I became less naïve, yet more hopeful; less controlling, yet more in control; less flexible in the ways that didn't serve me, yet more flexible where it did.

In addition, here is some information about the main tools I use, and which inform my approach in this book.

Ontological Coaching

You have most likely been exposed to those pithy aphorisms of the ancient or Eastern sages that people share as memes on Facebook. When you read them, the really good ones, you probably find yourself going, *Yes, that's so true.* In those moments, your mind goes quiet.

By contrast, when you are given information in the form of an academic lecture or text, your mind gets busy with thinking. Thinking leads to more thinking, and things can get quite noisy in your mind.

When your mind goes quiet, it's because you've had an insight—or a reminder—into the way things are without any interpretation that is based on historic, cultural, personal or intellectual bias. An insight cuts through subjective thinking, and knowledge-based learning, to see things as they are.

Ontological coaching is a method of questioning that delivers this type of insight, thick and fast, on the issues that you've been going around in circles analysing for months and years. It supports you to stop your normal spiral through delivering an insight and, in that space, to make plans to exit the spiral and set a new course.

The Enneagram

For the most part, our personalities are positive and, by expressing them, we can offer our gifts to the world. The problem is that those same personalities include what we call a defence mechanism: the things we've learned to avoid at all costs.

Some people avoid breaking the rules at all costs, while others avoid seeing them at all—they pretend the rules don't exist; some avoid risk at all costs, while others avoid failure at all costs; some avoid conflict at all costs, while others avoid people at all costs. We each have one or two key areas of avoidance which are constantly being triggered and send us spiralling into habitual patterns.

The enneagram is a tool that identifies your core gifts and avoidances, and links these to your habitual behavioural patterns. It joins the dots for you and for me as coach in a way that vastly accelerates the discovery phase of the coaching process, and deepens the conversation throughout.

Practical Mindfulness

Mindfulness has become a buzzword. Yet it's about so much more than just being present while you eat and walk. Applied properly, mindfulness is at the heart of all personal development.

The first step towards improving or transforming oneself is awareness, or being able to observe oneself objectively. This is easier said than done. When a person is angry, or scared, they are not likely to become aware. They tend to "lose themselves".

Mindfulness trains the mind to recognise when it's in a reactive state, to become present, and then to make a better choice about how to act in the situation. Clearly there are many ways to achieve this. However, mindfulness is like the "salt in the mix" that brings up the flavours of the dish—it enhances the gains you make through any other kind of practice or process.

To sum up, then, I specialise in coaching clients towards the practical application of mindfulness for optimal performance, a result which I call *Personal Effectiveness*. People high in personal effectiveness experience being authentic and successful, confident, caring and conscious, and powerful and peaceful.

Since all human endeavour is achieved through one's efforts in relation to other people, my sessions are always targeted at improved performance through a greater awareness of self in relationship with others. Converting insights into actions, and measuring those actions, is key. Developing practices to support the process embeds the new insights and actions as productive behaviour patterns.

Finally, it's important to state that great coaching is invisible. It leaves you feeling that you created the solution for yourself, and this is necessary for adoption and integration. It should not feel like work, but liberation. It should create independence and self-sufficiency, and leave you feeling inspired and having the tools to continue to grow.

About Personal Effectiveness

PERSONAL EFFECTIVENESS means having the personal power to consciously achieve optimal performance in service of your most meaningful goals while remaining present and peaceful in the midst of life's turbulence.

Let's unpack that a little.

You know that feeling when things aren't going your way? You're not getting the deal, or the sale, or the promotion you're after. You're not getting the woman, or the guy, you're after. You're promising to stop drinking, go on a diet, get back to gym, and you're not doing it. Despite all the best intentions and what seems like a great effort, life is running away from you. It feels more like you're driving in first or second gear: lots of revs and noise, and little movement.

Life comes at you hard and fast, and it keeps coming. And when you increase your personal power, you get those results, and more, with what feels like less effort. It's like you've moved into a higher gear. Or like you've got a long lever in your hand and you're at the right end of it! Yes, it is possible, and knowing more about yourself and about how to make life work for you —which is what this program is designed to teach—provides the key. Or, to stay with the metaphor, the lever.

The next little noteworthy statement in that sentence or definition is to "consciously achieve". Being conscious doesn't just mean that you eat organic and recycle your plastic. Being conscious means getting ahead of yourself, or getting on top of what we'll call your reactive self. Your reactive self is that part of you that gets angry in traffic, or doesn't think before acting. So instead of just blindly doing what everyone else is doing, you start to think about how you're going to respond. And that includes thinking about the direction your life is taking and making some deliberate choices in that regard.

Most people, when they become conscious in this way, tend to choose goals that are less self-serving and, instead, become more caring, more transcendent; they tend to want to be more honest, more authentic.

Optimal performance is that state of performance when you're at the top of your game, you're doing what you love, time seems to disappear, and everything seems to be going your way. That state of performance—and the factors for creating it—has been studied scientifically. The factors are known, they're under your conscious control and so you can replicate them if you know how. You can achieve this at both micro, or task, level and at a macro, or lifestyle, level.

Then we come to your most meaningful goals. Sure, we all want to make money and provide for our families, and to be respected socially and professionally. Then, beyond that, there are often things that matter just as much, or, sometimes, even more. Like raising happy, balanced, successful children. Or being fit and healthy. Or making a real contribution to the world, leaving a legacy. Carl Jung and Victor Frankl both agree: meaning is more important and more powerful motivator than just happiness. Making sure that your goals are meaningful is the key to making sure you stick with them when the going gets tough.

Finally, being present and peaceful in the midst of life's turbulence. Isn't that what it's all about? Anyone who has achieved a significant goal will tell you that that achievement is momentary. Very soon, you start looking around for the next thing. If you kill yourself to get there, you're effectively giving up all the moments of your life for the sake of one moment, which is ultimately not satisfying. Making sure that you're present and peaceful along the journey to any goal is surely the most rational choice you can make. Plus, when you're operating in that state, you make better decisions based on what's real and what matters, and so that completes the circle of personal power.

When you put all of this together, you can see why I say that people high in personal effectiveness experience being authentic and successful, confident, caring and conscious, and powerful and peaceful.

OK, so what are you waiting for? Let's get started!

1 | Getting Motivated

IMAGINE YOU overheard two people talking about going to climb a mountain, say, Kilimanjaro. You might think about it once or twice the next day, but then you'll probably forget about it. On the other hand, imagine that you woke up one morning and remembered that you'd sworn a blood oath with your best friend to climb Kilimanjaro within the next six months!

If you were serious about keeping your promise, you'd have a whole new set of thoughts occurring in your mind, wouldn't you? The first few thoughts might be horror and dread, but then you'd start to think about what you need. Flights. Equipment. Training.

You'd probably start doing research online. You'd learn things you never would have otherwise. You may even notice that there's a hiking shop at the mall, one that you've passed a hundred times without even paying any attention to it. Now, you're in there, talking fine details about hiking boots.

The point is that when you commit to achieve something, your mind immediately starts sending signals to you about what you'll need in order to achieve that. Conversely, when you just heard a conversation about it, and made no decision about it, you didn't think about it again.

If you want to get the best out of your reading of this book—or anything in life, for that matter—then you should define some outcomes for your participation, as you're about to do, and then commit to achieve them. In this way you're taking responsibility for your participation.

Instead of just being spoon-fed, you actively engage in getting your questions answered. Your mind will then naturally focus on, and pay attention to, the things you need as and when they come up—not only during the sessions, but in your daily life in between the sessions too.

So go ahead and do that exercise now!

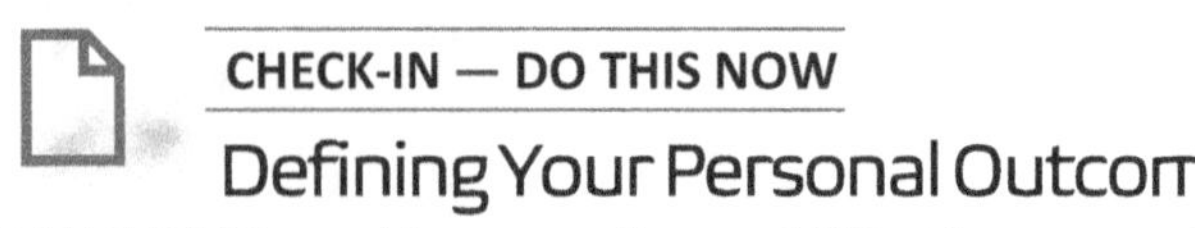

CHECK-IN — DO THIS NOW

Defining Your Personal Outcomes

WHAT DOES coaching mean for you? What brings you to this book? What do you hope to get out of it? By setting clear objectives, your mind will send signals to you about what to look out for and guide you to focus on what's important for you. Use these questions to guide you to set clear objectives in order to maximise your learning while reading this book.

Question 1 (of 3) What are the three main areas of challenge you are currently experiencing, where you think coaching can help? (For example, "I'm frustrated / bored / depressed and so I eat / drink / exercise too much," or, "I can't seem to get on the right career track," or, "My life has no enjoyment / purpose / meaning," etc.)

1)

2)

3)

Question 2 (of 3) What are the obstacles you've experienced when you've tried to make changes to these in the past? (For example, "I try hard, but I just can't seem to get the results I want," or, "I took some chances and things didn't work out," or, "I have no idea what I want or how to make the changes I need to make.")

1)
2)
3)

Question 3 (of 3) Now try to imagine how you would behave, or how your life would look, in those three scenarios if you could have things exactly as you'd want them. Describe them as objectively as possible. (For example, "I'd stick to my diet and exercise plan and only deviate once a month," or, "I'll have a written, realistic plan to get the position / business I want," or, "I'll be 100% clear about what's important for me and know what I need to do to be on the right path," etc.) Make your outcome specific and measurable.

1) Transfer to Main Goal **[A]**
2) Transfer to Main Goal **[B]**
3) Transfer to Main Goal **[C]**

My Main Goal: Outcomes Statement

USE THIS table to record three main outcomes, or goals, that you hope for—and are prepared to commit to—while reading this book. Do this by transferring the "perfect scenario" statements that you made in response to Question 3 on the previous page into this table.

Goal	Measurable outcome
(A)	Write your main goal as a measurable outcome into this space. ☐ Commit to achieve?
(B)	Write your main goal as a measurable outcome into this space. ☐ Commit to achieve?
(C)	Write your main goal as a measurable outcome into this space. ☐ Commit to achieve?

KEY CONCEPT — TAKE NOTE
Motivational States

WE CAN identify five motivational states, which are distinct from moods or emotions in that they're more stable and more directly under your conscious control—if you know how. These states are:

- Agitation (using force, not getting anywhere)
- Flow (enjoyment, absorption, the loss of time)
- Animation (positive mental or physical action towards a goal)
- Rest (active relaxation, recovery)
- Ennui (boredom, resistance)

Flow Think about those times when you're doing something you love, like your favourite hobby. If you're a musician, it's when you're in the groove. Or, for those exercise bunnies, it's when you're hitting those peak performance levels. In those moments, you lose track of time, forget all your worries and feel exhilarated. We call that the "flow" state, or the state of "optimal experience". The flow state has been studied scientifically over decades. The factors that are present, and which are needed for you to get into that state, are actually under your conscious control. At a later stage we'll take a look at those factors.

Rest After a good bit of activity, you're going to want to rest. Rest is good, if it's deliberate, consciously chosen rest for the sake of recovery.

Ennui If you remain in the state of rest for too long, you're likely to drop down into the state of ennui, or boredom. When you're bored, like on a Sunday when you've been lying around all day, you don't feel like getting going, do you? It becomes a self-reinforcing—or self-destructive—spiral.

Animation When you start out with any activity—even one that you enjoy—you often don't feel like it. For example, when you start out on your run, or when you get up off the couch to start work on that project. It feels like a huge effort—at least until you get going. We'll call this the state of animation. It's that state of active engagement—that phase of "getting going"—where you're making the effort even though you don't feel like it. Animation can be activated by an external force, for example your boss gave you a deadline, or internally, where you make a choice to shift your own lazy ass for your own reasons, for your own good.

Agitation Then, of course, there are those times when you're pushing too hard to make things happen. You're pushing too hard against life. Trying to do more, or do things faster, than reality will allow. Like when you're stuck in the traffic and it's not going to shift for you, no matter how much you scream and shout. You get angry, irritable and frustrated. We'll call this the state of agitation.

Now, a special word on getting started, and getting into the animated state.

Think about nuclear energy. It can be used constructively, or destructively. The same with fire. Constructive or destructive. In both instances, when these energies are being used positively, you'll find that they're contained, rather than unleashed. For example, a nuclear reactor that powers a city (contained) versus a nuclear bomb that destroys one (uncontained). Or a fire in a hearth (contained) versus a forest fire (uncontained). It's the same with your life energy. You can harness it and contain it, and use it constructively, or you can let it get out of control.

How do you create a container so that you can consciously activate and positively harness your life force energy? The simple answer is, by making a decision to get into the animated state and then acting on that decision! Of course, there's more to it than that and so we'll address this point in more detail again in later chapters.

THE SCIENCE / THE SOURCE

The Pursuit of Happiness

THE SCIENTIFIC studies referred to on the previous page were led by Mihály Csikszentmihalyi (pronounced *shik-shent-mee-hal-yee*), former professor of psychology at the University of Chicago. He published his results in 1992, in the form of a book called *Flow: The Psychology of Happiness*. You'll learn more about his findings later in this program. For now, read this summary of his reflections on the nature and the source of happiness.

In the introduction to the first chapter of his book, Csikszentmihalyi points out that his "discovery" was that "happiness is not

something that happens. It is not the
result of good fortune or random chance. It is not something that
money can buy or power command. It does not depend on outside events, but, rather, on how we interpret them."

This confirms what the Greco-Roman philosophical school, the
Stoics, said two thousand years ago. They held the view that "our
feelings about life's events, not those events themselves, determine our happiness".

Csikszentmihalyi adds that, "Happiness, in fact, is a condition that
must be prepared for, cultivated, and defended privately by each
person. People who learn to control inner experience will be able
to determine the quality of their lives, which is as close as any of
us can come to being happy.

"Yet we cannot reach happiness by consciously searching for it.
'Ask yourself whether you are happy,' said J.S. Mill, 'and you cease
to be so.' It is by being fully involved with every detail of our lives,
whether good or bad, that we find happiness, not by trying to
look for it directly.

"Victor Frankl, the Austrian psychologist, summarized it beauti-
fully in the preface to his book *Man's Search for Meaning*: 'Don't
aim at success—the more you aim at it and make it a target, the
more you are going to miss it. For success, like happiness, cannot
be pursued; it must ensue … as the unintended side-effect of
one's personal dedication to a course greater than oneself.'[To
achieve this] elusive goal that cannot be attained by a direct
route, we have to take a circuitous path that begins with [gaining]
control over the contents of our consciousness.

"[We] have all experienced times when … we do feel in control of
our actions … we feel a sense of exhilaration … that becomes a
landmark memory for what life should be like. This is termed
optimal experience. Such events do not occur only when the external conditions are favourable. Sometimes—often—these occur, surprisingly, in the midst of [an] ordeal, such as a near-fatal
physical danger.

> "The best moments in our lives are not the passive, receptive, relaxing times... The best moments usually occur when a person's body or mind is stretched to its limits in a voluntary effort to accomplish something difficult and worthwhile. Optimal experience is thus something that we make happen.
>
> "Such experiences are not necessarily pleasant at the time they occur. [For example, the swimmer's lungs and muscles, which hurt whenever they train towards a greater goal.] Getting control of life is never easy, and sometimes it can be definitely painful. But in the long run optimal experiences add up to a sense of mastery—or, perhaps better, a sense of participation in determining the content of life—that comes as close to what is usually meant by happiness as anything else we can conceivably imagine."

If you're still here, well done. You've made it past the first challenge, which is to recognise that this process is going to involve a fair bit of deliberate, conscious effort on your part. It's not a free ride. If achieving your goals was easy, then coaching wouldn't be a thing, and you wouldn't be here. You'd already be on that desert island, or sailing that yacht, or whatever it is that you dream about. Now let's move on and take this understanding further.

REAL-LIFE EXAMPLE

Making the Most of a Bad Situation

THE TERM "autotelic" derives from two Greek words: *auto* meaning self, and *telos* meaning goal. It refers to a self-contained activity, one that is done not with the expectation of some future benefit, but simply because the doing itself is the reward. Playing the stock market in order to make money is not an autotelic experience; but playing it in order to prove one's skill at foretelling future trends is—even though the outcome in terms of dollars and cents is exactly the same.

An autotelic personality is someone who can set a goal and act on it and thereby find some intrinsic meaning and reward out of the activity. They can do this even with things that they are initially forced to do against their will. In particular, the traits that mark an autotelic personality are most clearly revealed by people who are able to turn harrowing conditions, like being lost in Antarctica, into a manageable and even enjoyable struggle—whereas most others would succumb to the ordeal.

Richard Logan, who has studied the accounts of many people in difficult situations, concludes that they survived by finding ways to turn the bleak objective conditions into subjectively controllable experience. In other words, they follow the blueprint of flow activities. You'll find out more about that blueprint later in this program. For now, what's important is to note that they paid close attention to the most minute details of their environment. Below are some examples.

Christopher Burney, a prisoner of the Nazis who spent a long time in solitary confinement during World War II, explained how they would take the few objects that they had and ask a whole catalogue of often absurd questions about them. Does it work? How? Who made it and of what? And so on. Then they moved on to more abstract references, like measuring each object in terms of the other one's qualities, and so on.

Essentially the same ingenuity in finding opportunities for mental action and setting goals is reported by survivors of any solitary confinement, from diplomats captured by terrorists, to elderly ladies imprisoned by Chinese communists. Eva Zeisel, the ceramic designer who was imprisoned in Moscow's Lubyanka prison for over a year by Stalin's police, kept her sanity by figuring out how she would make a bra out of materials at hand, playing chess against herself in her head, holding imaginary conversations in French, doing gymnastics, and memorising poems she composed. Alexander Solzhenitsyn describes how one of his fellow prisoners in the Lefortovo jail mapped the world on the floor of the cell and then imagined himself travelling across Asia and Europe to America, covering a few kilometres each day.

Albert Speer, Hitler's favourite architect, sustained himself in Spandau prison for months by pretending he was taking a walking trip from Berlin to Jerusalem, which is imagination provided all the events and sites along the way.

An acquaintance of Csikszentmihalyi who worked in United States Air Force intelligence tells the story of a pilot who was imprisoned in North Vietnam for many years and lost eighty pounds and much of his health in the jungle camp. When he was released, one of the first things he asked for was to play a game of golf. To the great astonishment of his fellow officers he played a superb game despite his emaciated condition. To their enquiries he replied that every day of his imprisonment he imagined himself playing 18 holes, carefully choosing his clubs and approach and systematically varying the course. This discipline not only helped preserve his sanity but apparently also kept his physical skills well honed.

When adversity threatens to paralyse us, we need to reassert control by finding a new direction in which to invest psychic energy, a direction that lies outside the reach of external forces. When every aspiration is frustrated, a person still must seek a meaningful goal around which to organise the self. Then, even though that person is objectively a slave, subjectively he is free."

—from *Flow: The Psychology of Happiness*
by Mihály Csikszentmihalyi

As you can see, it's not only about achieving a goal so that you can have better external circumstances. Yes, you want to live as comfortably and enjoyably as you can, and you should make every effort towards that. However, if that's the only goal, then, firstly, you miss the joy of the journey. (And since, for many people, getting to that ultimate goal takes a lot longer than they would like, so that journey that they miss out on turns out to be the better part of their lives.) Secondly, you miss the point. Because the point, surely, is not just to plant flags in the ground, but to become a better person while doing that.

Becoming a better person means gaining power over yourself as well as mastering your environment. It means to not be defined by your circumstances, but by your response to them. To not be defined by whether you achieve the goal or not, but by your efforts towards it and how you treat people and the world along the way. It means making the most of every moment of the journey, no matter how good, or how bad.

Here's what Eckhart Tolle has to say on the subject: "Make sure your vision or goal is not … focused on having this or that, such as a mansion by the sea, your own company, or ten million dollars in the bank. … [A] vision of yourself having this or that are all static goals and therefore don't empower you. Instead, make sure your goals are dynamic, that is to say, point toward an activity that you are engaged in and through which you are connected to other human beings as well as to the whole. Instead of seeing yourself as a famous actor and writer and so on, see yourself inspiring countless people with your work and enriching their lives. Feel how that activity enriches or deepens not only your life but that of countless others."

The point is not just to plant flags in the ground, but to become a better person while doing that.

What Tolle is pointing to there is the internal, qualitative experience, not the external quantitative one. When you can have the same rich, enjoyable and meaningful experience of life, no matter what your external circumstances, that's an indicator of what we'd call transformation, which is deeper than change. Change happens on the outside and is good. Transformation happens on the inside and is infinitely greater.

Tolle is also pointing to a sense of global connectedness—being connected to others, to the world, and to the ultimate purpose and impact of what you do. There's the story of the floor cleaner at NASA. The president visits the site and asks him, "What do you do?" He answers, "I help put people in space." He sees the bigger picture and feels connected. His work is meaningful, even though he's not the engineer or the astronaut who will appear at the press conference.

So, yes, by all means, you must have your goals, and can you be like that janitor on your way to achieving them? You're invited to always remember this as you work towards your main goals.

2 | Know Yourself

T'S IMPOSSIBLE to see your own eyes without a mirror. Similarly, you need a lens through which to see your own personality more objectively. In this chapter, you'll be introduced to a tool that can help you to do that. It's called the enneagram and it presents nine core personality styles, each one of which has a core main attribute, or gift, that you offer to the world. When you're acting in alignment with that style, you're more likely to enjoy what you're doing and get into the flow state. For example, some people are happiest when they're ticking off boxes; others when they're lifting people's spirits or presenting new and inspiring ideas; others when they're working alone, performing an in-depth task to a high standard. And so on.

You might be very clear on your answer to this, or you might be very unclear. Some people may agree with your perception of yourself; others may not. Some people may appreciate these things about you; others may not. Either way, you would probably find it useful to have a deeper understanding of yourself along these dimensions.

Chapter Theme Outcomes

Discover or learn more about your core personality attributes and how you can act in alignment with those to get into the flow state.

By engaging in this chapter you will:

- ✓ Discover a tool that will support you to recognise your dominant personality style(s);
- ✓ Recognise the gift that you bring to the world as a result of that personality style;
- ✓ Learn about the core defence mechanism or avoidance area that underlies that personality style;
- ✓ Know what activities you can undertake that are most likely to get you into the flow state or state of "optimal experience".

KEY CONCEPT — TAKE NOTE

The Enneagram

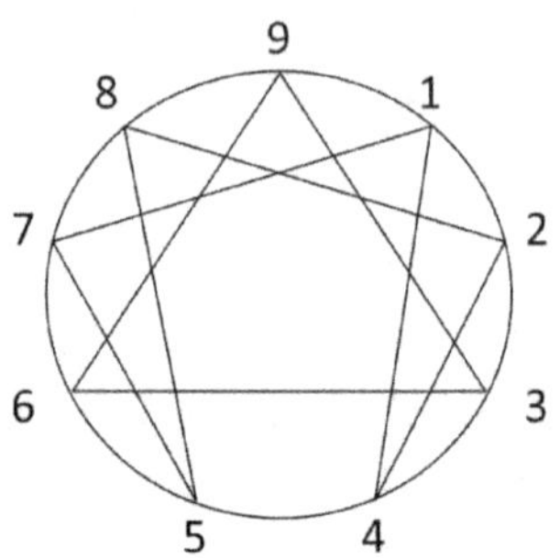

AN ENNEAGRAM (Greek: "picture of nine", or "nine points") is a mathematical model with ancient roots, dating back at least to the time of Pythagoras. It has certain rules of operation and you can apply a set of information to the model and get a neat, explanatory outcome. The enneagram of personality is one such outcome and it describes nine core personality "styles" or "types". (I'll use the term "style" which seems less restrictive—it doesn't put your personality in a box, which is what tends to happen when you refer to it as a "type".)

The great thing about the enneagram is that it doesn't just tell you "what" you are, but also "why" you are the way you are—in other words, what drives you. What drives you, according to the enneagram, is an underlying defence mechanism, which is also termed an "area of avoidance". This is an area of dislike or discomfort that develops in early childhood, as your unique reaction to your environment. Usually what happens is that you'll build a bit of a personality structure around that avoidance. For example, some might strive from an early age to avoid "negativity" at all costs, and so they'll make sure they're always seeking out the "positive". Others might avoid getting criticised for breaking the rules, being bad, or making a mistake, and so they'll make sure they always do what's "right".

With the enneagram you can become more flexible and develop a more integrated personality.

This is a simplistic description of the model. There is much more to it than that. In particular, a whole set of behaviours and attitudes is associated with each style. For example, the person who avoids "negativity" is also very likely to do their best to avoid following any rules, or paying attention to details, both of which they'll see as "negative". On the positive side, this can lead to them being quite enterprising, as well as inspiring and innovative. At their best that can be the visionaries like Richard Branson who lead people into uncharted territory. However, this same trait can lead to them being quite scattered and likely to avoid dealing with serious issues when they do arise. (Disclaimer: I don't know if that's true for Mr Branson, but I doubt it.)

Conversely, the person who avoids criticism will strive for perfect and ethical behaviour and make it their mission to enforce the rules. On the positive side, this type of person will lead everybody to raise their game. On the downside, they can be very strict and critical, to the point of being restrictive and even damaging people's creativity and self-esteem.

In addition, you can see the kinds of conflicts that might arise between the above two styles, especially when they're not aware of themselves and therefore driven to express their avoidances at the extreme, at all costs.

An understanding of the enneagram can enable people to become more flexible around their key avoidances and therefore to develop a more integrated personality. This can lead to a more realistic and productive approach to life, particularly in terms of interpersonal relationships.

There are various tests you can do online to determine your own enneagram style. Some are more accurate—and more expensive—than others. I offer one, along with a debrief, via my website. You can also do a fairly good job of working out your own enneagram style just by reading about them. You'll get a chance to do that later on in this chapter.

THE SCIENCE / THE SOURCE

The Enneagram and Psychological Models

ATTEMPTS TO classify human behaviour and temperament have been around since the time of Hippocrates in ancient Greece. He attempted to attribute the differences between the four recognised "types" accepted at the time to, inter alia, the seasons and to body fluids. However, there was still a randomness that eluded him. The Chinese, through the *I Ching*, classified people according to the elements.

One of the most significant advances in human thinking may be ascribed to Sir Isaac Newton, who became the advocate of a new scientific view of the world which, although mechanistic, enabled phenomena to be measured, quantified and understood in mathematical terms. This led, much further down the line, to the emergence of formal psychometric instruments. The first of these was initiated in 1885 at Cambridge University in the form of anthropometrics. Later on, through Stanford University, came Binet's well-known Intelligence Quotient (IQ).

This evolved into tests that set out to measure temperament, and these may be divided into two broad categories: (a) observation-based measures, which start from a premise of no knowledge and allow the broad data they collect to reveal its secrets; and (b) theory-based measures, which go out to confirm the existence of a hypothesised difference between people. The former are known as typological models; the latter, trait models.

People are qualitatively more complex than the typological or the trait theories can ever hope to assess, and neither type nor traits can define the person as a whole. In addition, there seems little purpose in pointing out differences unless they actually mean something, which implies the subject being able to do something practically with the information. If they are based on some factor over which the subject has little or no control, they can be used by that person to label themselves and become a victim of the "typing". They can also be used by others to discriminate against the person who has been labelled.

The enneagram is a possible candidate for an elegant, yet simple, way of describing human individual differences that satisfies both the typological and trait theorists. It is neither exclusively a trait model nor a type model, but both, depending on the vantage point from which you view it. It also provides practical insights and a development path for the individual.

The person credited with doing the most to bring the enneagram into a credible alignment with western scientific thinking is Claudio Naranjo, who was born in Chile and trained as a psychiatrist in the USA. He aligned the model with the principles of personality psychology and the DSM-III, the index of psychiatric and personality disorders. This material formed the basis of his first book,

Character and Neurosis, which is still considered to be the master-work on the Enneagram

A more recent paper by Jenna Talbott of the University of Denver, published in DU Portfolio, October 2015, describes each of the nine Enneagram personality types in connection with one (or two) of the DSM-IV-TR personality disorders. The similarities between the unhealthy tendencies of each type and the descriptions of the personality disorders are emphasized.

A 2005 Occupational Personality Questionnaire (OPQ) correlative study on the Enneagram by Anna Brown and Dave Bartram makes further links to current models.

It's worth noting that the enneagram is sometimes regarded in the corporate sphere as being associated with New Age woo-woo. This is mostly because nobody knows where it came from. It didn't come from Freud or Jung, so the psychological community immediately frowns on it—they don't seem to mind that those two men's ideas were and continue to be largely untested by the scientific method. It's certainly not based on astrology or numerology or anything like that. Its origins remain lost in the mists of time.

However, it's gaining more and more currency in the mainstream as it gets subjected to more and more scientific testing and validation—and as more and more people experience it and testify to just how well it describes them. There's every probability that will continue to pass many more of those tests and will emerge as one of the most accurate and comprehensive descriptors of human behaviour.

REAL-LIFE EXAMPLE

Getting the "One" in Me

I FIRST encountered the enneagram many years ago. I was browsing in a bookstore while waiting for my son to finish his ice hockey practice. The name "enneagram" itself, and the disc with its colours and lines, looked and felt strangely familiar, yet I knew nothing about it. I had trained to deliver a number of personality profiles, and found them useful, so I flipped through the book. The nature of the descriptions led me to conclude that it might be another New Age horoscope-type tool that promised a lot but delivered little. I put it back.

Later on, a colleague suggested I take an enneagram test. She said she sometimes used it with her clients and found it useful in pinpointing issues. She directed me to one of the more popular online tests. I completed the online questionnaire and received the results.

I came out as being dominant in the style number One. The main attribute of this style is being a person who is overtly all about morals, ethics, standards and quality. We all have an element of this, but for the One it sits on top of everything else. It becomes paramount, potentially even an obsession. They send you back to fix a spelling error and point out all the rules. They can be experienced as quite harsh and critical.

I have great confidence that the enneagram is the sharpest tool in the personality profiling shed.

The enneagram says that these people—the Ones, like me—have that focus of attention precisely because their "area of avoidance" is to not make mistakes, not get things wrong, not do bad things and, most of all, to not be criticised. Therefore, the word criticism becomes a very sharp descriptor of what they avoid—and what they do. The words "right" and "wrong" appear prominently in their language.

When I heard all of this, it connected a thousand dots. A lot of my life suddenly made sense. I was very ethical and rule-driven, sometimes to my detriment. I could spot a spelling mistake from across the room. Plus, people have often experienced me as harsh and critical. I had lived a very Spartan lifestyle and denied myself many things that other people considered normal.

My interest was piqued, and I paid a lot more attention. The enneagram made a lot of sense, explained a lot of things, and seemed to be unusually accurate. I say this based not only on my own experience, but from the client feedback I gained after I completed a training and began to debrief people. Many clients were equally surprised by the accuracy with which it described them. This is not to mention the scientific research that I started to find online and the statistical analysis which the business whose reports I was using had done while developing its own model, and which I gained access to.

Later on, I started asking my clients a particular opening question. I made sure it was not a leading question, but a neutral one, and that I asked it in the same way every time. The results were fascinating. Almost without fail, at least one word or phrase *within the first sentence* of my clients' answers matched their dominant enneagram style as it appeared in the report that I had seen, and which they had not.

Later, I started to see that each style used a very small range of phrases, or set of key words, and, with some styles, it was one single word.

Today, I have great confidence that the enneagram is the sharpest tool in the personality profiling shed.

KEY CONCEPT — TAKE NOTE

The Enneagram & Flow

LET'S LOOK at your personality style, in terms of the enneagram and how that relates to the subject of motivational states—in particular, the state of flow. What you might find is that when you are acting in alignment with your dominant enneagram style, that you more naturally and easily get into the flow state.

As mentioned, the enneagram describes nine core personality styles, each one of which, despite its "area of avoidance", has a mostly positive side—the thing that you like doing which also becomes a gift or attribute that you can offer the world. When you're working in alignment with that attribute, you'll most naturally and easily get into the flow state. So, let's take a look at those now and see if you can identify your one, perhaps two, dominant styles.

NOTE The "red zone" is that state you get into when your core fear or "area of avoidance" has been triggered. There'll be a whole chapter about the "red zone" later in the program (Chapter 9). For now, just to know that it's the opposite of your happy place.

Style #1 | Working to improve / perfect things

The Style #1's red zone would most likely be triggered if they were expected to do something that breaks the rules or goes against procedures or best practice. On the contrary, they might find that their gift, and what's most likely to get them into the flow state, is when they are working to improve or perfect things. For example, finding a better, more efficient or neater way to do something. This may include defining and/or refining processes. It could also extend to auditing compliance to those processes. This strong desire for constant improvement, even perfection, as well as adherence to rules and quality standards might be extrapolated into other forms or expression too. For example, it might show up as campaigning to get people to adhere to a higher standard of morals or ethics.

Style #2 | Helping others do practical things

For the Style #2, their red zone would be triggered if they believed they were being seen to be selfish or seen to be putting themselves first. Conversely, they might find that the gift that they offer to the world, and what's most likely to get them into the flow state, is when they are helping others to solve problems, finish tasks or with anything that the other person may need. They tend to be quite practical in their approach and are likely to get absorbed in doing stuff for other people. If they benefit indirectly, then great, but of primary importance is that they're serving others and helping other people meet their needs.

Style #3 | Achieving and building reputation

For the Style #3, the red zone would be triggered if they believed that some current or possible future event could lead to them being seen as a failure or potentially suffering reputational damage. Conversely, the gift that they offer to the world, and what would get them into the flow state most naturally and easily, is when they are identifying and working on—or, more likely, managing other people to work on—projects that will lead to some form of social or professional recognition. They may also be driven by financial reward, but that would only be to the extent that it can enhance their social status, for example by enabling them to buy a car that would impress future clients. They would also be likely to get into the flow state while presenting a project that they believe will succeed or one that has been successful.

Style #4 | Doing stuff that is unique and meaningful

For the Style #4, the red zone would be triggered if they believed that they were being asked to do something that would be humdrum, or ordinary in the sense that it had no meaning or that it did not recognise their unique talents and creativity. Conversely, their gift to the world, and what's most likely to get them into the flow state, is when they are, for example, using their unique talents to create something original and aesthetically pleasing, as well as meaningful. This could mean artistic endeavours like art, design, music or writing, and it could be in more commercial endeavours. The key being that the project that is truly meaningful to them and that their contribution harnesses and recognises their uniqueness and originality.

Style #5 | Reading and researching

For the Style #5, the five red zone would be triggered if they believed they were being made to look or feel stupid in a social situation, especially by having to make an impromptu speech on a subject they feel they don't know enough about, or making small talk. As you can see, for them it's all about knowledge, and knowing stuff. As such, their gift to the world, and what's most likely to get them into the flow state, is when they are gathering knowledge. In other words, reading or doing research and gathering data or writing up and analysing that data. Preferably in a solitary environment where they can be removed from public interaction. You can think of scientists in their labs, researchers and writers, or computer programmers in dark rooms being fed pizza under the door!

Style #6 | Contingency planning

For the Style #6, the red zone would be triggered if they were asked to do something that they saw as dangerous and risky without being able to plan properly. Conversely, their gift to the world, and entry point into the flow state, is when they are scenario planning. This personality style is also able to keep a cool head in an emergency, mostly because they've researched and thought about what to do. So they're quite likely to find their flow state when working in any kind of emergency field.

Style #7 | Exploring, inspiring, communicating

For the Style #7, the red zone would be triggered if they believed they were being constrained by rules or perceived negativity. Conversely, their gift to the world, and entry point into the flow state, is when they are out in the world, exploring new ideas and possibilities, preferably combined with some fun activity like socialising. It could also be when they're communicating those new possibilities to people in a way that those others might become enthused to take on the ideas and execute them. Because, after all, for them the execution is, like, so boring!

Style #8 | Doing and being in charge

For the Style #8, the red zone would be triggered if they believed they were being made to be vulnerable or found themselves not in control of their own destiny. Conversely, their gift to the world, and what's most likely to get them into the flow state, is when they are in charge of the practical aspects of a project. This can show up as micromanaging. However, in its more positive expression, it can show up as being a champion who leads a group of people to fearlessly take on the world. A bit like Mandela did.

Style #9 | Harmonising

For the Style #9, the red zone would be triggered if they found themselves caught in conflict, with the perceived possibility of losing relationship as a result of that conflict. Conversely, their gift to the world, and what's most likely to get them into the flow state, is when they are reading the room for conflict and helping people to resolve it. In other words, when they're acting as an arbitrator or mediator. In addition, while some people may rebel against routine, the 9's are likely to enjoy just quietly getting on with any job.

Hopefully you managed to find yourself in all of that. For some, it will have been easy and obvious. Something will jump out at you. Some may find that they can relate to more than one style. That's OK too. You may have two styles that are quite dominant, occasionally even three. If that's the case, you'd need to do some more in-depth work with the tool to determine which style is most dominant.

Having that information about the positive attribute of your personality, you can start to see why you tend to do things in the way that you do. It feels good, it feels safe, it feels right. That's great and you should use that. Allow yourself to do more of those things, or to align your work and your hobbies with those kinds of activities. If it's not what you get to do in your formal job, then how can you make it so? Or how can you let people know that you're the go-to person for seeing the opportunity in any situation, or for assessing projects for their levels of risk, and so on? Truth be told, other people have probably already figured that out about you!

While you're doing those things you enjoy and are good at, you might then begin to invite and/or welcome others to fill in the gaps. If you look around you, you might identify some of the other personality styles based on the enneagram and start to figure out how you can work better together. To do that properly, you may want to explore the enneagram in greater depth. There are many books and online resources available.

You might choose to express that gift or attribute in
ways that can help and inspire people.

Or it might be to start expressing more of the positive side of your personality style. In other words, expressing that gift or attribute in ways that can help and inspire people, instead of being all about avoiding that thing that triggers you and sends you into the red zone. So if you're the Style 8, for example, how could you use all that power and virility to champion a cause "out there" rather than to micromanage the people in your inner circle in order to avoid not being in control?

Or if you're the Style 2, how can you take care of your own deadlines first, before you get busy helping everybody else? Or for the Style 6, perhaps you can see that yours is the contingency plan, not the only plan.

We tend to view the world through our own lens and, often without realising it, expect the rest of the world to see things and do things the way that we do. If you overplay your hand in terms of your enneagram style, you're bound to get that as feedback from your world, especially from those close to you. By recognising that your way is just your way and not the absolute truth, you can take your foot off the gas a bit in terms of being you. You can start to let others in, to celebrate differences, to see other possibilities for how you can be. And, when doing this, as you'll learn in Chapter 9 on the red zone, to recognise that you don't die!

3 | Working with Values

YOUR VALUES are the most important determinant of the decisions you make. In fact, you always make decisions in line with your most important values. Your decisions move you forward in life and, since your life is likely to involve other people, those decisions will often put you in conflict with others. Or you might find that you don't make decisions for fear of that fact.

This chapter will enable you to rank your set of values and see how that particular ranking impacts the decisions you make and how you order and prioritise things in your life. You'll also see how that in turn impacts your relationships and, in particular, your typical areas of conflict with other people. If you're avoiding making decisions, it might show you what decisions you would make if you'd let yourself.

Chapter Theme Outcomes

Discover or learn more about your priority of values and how that impacts both the decisions you consistently make and your views of, and relationships with, other people.

By engaging in this chapter you will:

- ✓ Discover what really matters most to you and why you organise your life the way you do;
- ✓ Recognise the source of many of your behavioural patterns and conflicts with other people;
- ✓ Learn to gather evidence about, and come to terms with, what matters to you;
- ✓ Know how to be more flexible and have more choice with regards to how you make decisions and respond to the world.

Working with Values

REMEMBER THE Kilimanjaro example? It shows how ideas are born out of other ideas. You can say that decisions are a particular form of idea—a choice—born out of another particular form of idea—a fixed idea called a belief. Those beliefs are based on what you value most. For example, you might value family more than money—or vice versa—or knowledge and learning more than being fit and healthy.

Decisions are generally congruent with what you value most—whether you realise it or not. Therefore, when presented with a choice of a job that makes you twice as much money, but it means you'll be far from your family, you might find it easy to say yes, or you may well turn down the job. Your decision will be based on—and will provide evidence for—what you value most: money or family.

Or you might find yourself with a dilemma, being torn between the two and unable to decide. This would mean that you don't know what you value most, or that you can't admit it to yourself—you feel guilty, or somehow lack permission. Finally, you may take the job and convince yourself that it's for your family—you'll be able to fly home or fly them to visit you. In this case, you're quite possibly not being honest with yourself—or them.

Whichever of those is you, you'll probably find it's not just true for one decision, but for most, if not every, decision you make and have ever made. In other words, you've consistently decided to sacrifice making money for the sake of family, or vice versa. Or you were consistently undecided between the two, and tended to do what you were expected to do, or wait until someone made the decision for you. Or you consistently chose the job and convinced yourself it was to serve the family, but chances are you're a bit behind on making it up to them.

Dr John Demartini says, "The only thing we are truly committed to is our [highest priority] values." This is reflected, not by what we say, but by the facts: where we spend our time, money, energy and attention—and the decisions we make. For example, if you decide to spend more evenings and weekends working than with your family, you're expressing your priority of values through those actions, regardless of what you might profess verbally about your family being the most important thing in your life. It's tough, but it's true. And yes, for ease of use, values can be categorised according the areas of life.

Work-life balance is another subject that emerges out of the values theme. When you do the exercise, you'll probably find that there are some areas of neglect. Perhaps you've been neglecting your health, or your social life. One thing you can be sure about is that whatever you neglect will eventually become the only thing that matters. For example, when you're sick, the only thing that matters is getting better.

That said, I'm not an advocate of balance so much as being clear about your values. Clarity of values is important for knowing who you are and for effective decision-making. So don't neglect any area, but also don't drive yourself crazy trying to do "balance".

Below is an exercise that you can use to determine your priority of values.

PRACTICAL EXERCISE — DO THIS NOW

Working with Values

USE THE table on the next page to score your values, then rank them in order of priority. When completing the table, ask yourself:

How much do I prioritise each area by planning and/or spending time and/or money and/or mental energy on this area of life? Do I sacrifice time / money / energy spent on other areas for the sake of this area? Score towards 1 if low; towards 10 if very high, then rank them from 1 to 8.

NOTE If you're in a job you love, and you'd stay regardless of how much you earn, you can mark **Meaningful Vocation** as high, even if you do earn well. If you're in a job you don't love, but you do it for the money—even if that money is intended to set you free so you can follow your passion—then you'd give **Meaningful Vocation** a lower score than **Making Money**.

You can score **Immediate Family / Significant Other** as higher than **Making Money** only if you've proved that you sacrifice your earnings—eg. by moving to a lower-paid job—specifically to spend time with them, even if all or most of your money is spent on them. It's tough, but it's true.

My Priority of Values

Values Ranking Table	
Area of Life Priority Score	Ranking
Health / Exercise / Diet / Fitness (Time / money / energy spent keeping fit / healthy) 1 2 3 4 5 6 7 8 9 10	Ranking:
Immediate Family / Significant Other* (Priority given to time with family / partner) 1 2 3 4 5 6 7 8 9 10	Ranking:
Social Life (Time and money spent socialising) 1 2 3 4 5 6 7 8 9 10	Ranking:
Spiritual Pursuits (Time and money spent on spiritual pursuits) 1 2 3 4 5 6 7 8 9 10	Ranking:
Intellectual Pursuits / Learning (Time and money spent educating yourself) 1 2 3 4 5 6 7 8 9 10	Ranking:
Meaningful Vocation (Time spent on work that is your passion, you do it regardless of money) 1 2 3 4 5 6 7 8 9 10	Ranking:
Making Money (Priority given to work that is primarily aimed at earning money) 1 2 3 4 5 6 7 8 9 10	Ranking:
Leisure (Time / money spent on travel and other leisure pursuits) 1 2 3 4 5 6 7 8 9 10	Ranking:

The first thing you may notice about your priority of values is that you are quite likely to feel guilty about what you really value, at least according to the evidence of how you spend your time, money, attention and energy. You may feel—as do most people who do this exercise—that you should value family, or friends, for example, more than you do. So if you're struggling with this, read on.

Here's what Anthony Robbins says about values in *Awaken the Giant Within*: "If we are not clear about what's most important in our lives—what we truly stand for—then how can we ever expect to lay the foundation for a sense of self-esteem, much less have the capacity to make effective decisions? If you've ever found yourself in a situation where you had a tough time making a decision about something, the reason is that you weren't clear about what you value most within that situation. We must remember that all decision-making comes down to values clarification.

"All decision-making comes down to
values clarification." — Anthony Robbins

"When you know what's important to you, making a decision is quite simple. Most people, though, are unclear about what's most important in their lives, and this decision-making becomes a form of internal torture. This is not true for those who've clearly defined the highest principles of their lives.

"Who are the most universally admired and respected people in [your] culture? Aren't they those who have a solid grasp of their own values, people who not only profess their standards, but live by them?"

As you can see, getting clear on what you value and ordering the areas of your life should not just be done in order to achieve work-life balance. It provides the foundation for who you are in the world and for the decisions you make. It's not something to feel guilty about or apologise for. That just wastes energy and does not lead to greater effectiveness. If you're still not convinced, jump forward to the real-life example of Nelson Mandela later in this chapter. Perhaps that will convince you to embrace your set of values wholeheartedly and live your life without apology.

That doesn't mean you can't reprioritise your values. In fact, here's an exercise for you to do just that. First, transfer your values from the previous table into the left-hand column of the table on the next page, ordered according to their ranking. If you choose to reprioritise them, write your adjusted priority of values into the right-hand column of the table below. **NOTE** Be careful not to delude yourself when reordering your priority of values. It's unlikely that your most important value, especially one that's been that way for your whole life to date, is suddenly going to take a back seat or drop right down the list. It's more likely that you'll bring up some lower order values to number two or three position, at a close second or third, than completely usurping your number one value.

My Priority of Values	
Original	Re-ordered
1.	
2.	
3.	
4.	
5.	
6.	
7.	
8.	

By now you should be getting an idea of just how strong your values are. In fact, they're so strong, that most people will rather die than give up their most important values. Nelson Mandela was prepared to die, nobly, for his values. Others may, less nobly, allow their values to drive them to death. Think about the man who dies of a heart attack while climbing the corporate ladder. Or the one who commits suicide when he loses his money, or reputation. Then there's the mother who forgoes a career or any sort of a "life" for the sake of her kids.

And if it's not quite that bad, it's close enough. Consider, for example, those scenes you get in the movies, like the one where the father misses his child's birthday because he's working late. He doesn't just do it once, does he? He does it again and again until his wife leaves him. In fact, you can say that we tend to make the same decision again and again, each time with different content, throughout our lives. In other words, each time that guy misses his kid's birthday party, the situation seems to justify it and he has a story based on the situation. What he's not seeing is the pattern of how he's deciding, unconsciously, based on his priority of values.

You can go so far as to say that you always, literally always, make decisions in line with your priority of values. Until you become conscious of this fact, that is. Then, as in the previous exercise, you can start to realign your priority of values and develop some flexibility around your highest values.

THE SCIENCE / THE SOURCE

The Neuroscience of Values

ADVANCES IN cognitive science provide an alternative, empirically plausible account of the nature of values. Values are mental processes that are both cognitive and emotional. They combine cognitive representations such as concepts, goals, and beliefs with emotional attitudes that have positive or negative valence. For example, the values associated with life and death require the mental concepts of life and death and also the emotional attitudes that view life as positive and death as negative.

Advances in neuroscience are making it plausible that such mental states are neural processes that combine cognition and emotion. Concepts operate in the brain as patterns of firing, in populations of neurons, that can work to classify objects and also make general inferences about them. Such neural representations are continuously bound with emotional activity—carried out by populations of neurons in brain areas such as the amygdala, ventral striatum, and ventromedial prefrontal cortex. From this perspective, values are neural processes resulting from binding cognitive representations of concepts, goals, and beliefs together with emotional attitudes.

— Paul Thagard Ph.D., What Are Values?, *Psychology Today*, 16 April 2013: https://www.psychologytoday.com/us/blog/hot-thought/201304/what-are-values

If you're not conscious of your priority of values and their power, they can run—and sometimes destroy—your life. So despite what Anthony Robbins has said, and despite the Mandela example later in this chapter, you'll probably still want to bring come conscious awareness to the way you live out your values. You probably don't want to continue being that guy who misses his child's birthday party every year, but who now just has a better justification for it. You'll probably want to use this knowledge and awareness to live your values strongly, and yet to be consciously flexible around them too. You'll want to use what you've learned to let go now and again and, yes, find some balance.

REAL-LIFE EXAMPLE

The Essence of Mandela's "Madiba Magic"

NELSON MANDELA is one of the most revered statesmen and leaders of the last century. He was very charismatic, and his charm was often referred to, using his affectionate clan name, as the "Madiba Magic". However, it wasn't just his charm that won him universal respect. Perhaps the primary attribute that earned him that admiration was his level of clarity of values, and his degree of adherence to those values.

You can view his life from a number of angles. Firstly, according to some people's standards, he can be said to have "failed" horribly as a husband and father. After all, he was hardly ever home. Firstly, he was in jail for 27 years. Seriously, how many people would shrink back from joining a political struggle for fear of what it would mean in terms of not being home for their family?

Once again, there's no judgement here. We're just looking at what is. After all, even before he went to prison, Mandela was often on the run from the security police. And prior to that, he was out rallying people to the cause. In fact, his late ex-wife Winnie has been quoted as having said, "To be with him was to be without him."

If he had been on a modern-day leadership program that talked about work-life balance, he would probably have laughed. He was clear on his values of social transformation (his meaningful vocation), and he had no hesitation in putting these first, even if it meant putting his life at risk, let alone time with his family.

During the Rivonia Trial, in which he was ultimately sentenced to life in prison, he expressed the famous statement that he was prepared to die for his cause of a non-racial society.

This was not the kind of willingness to die that most people have when they unconsciously let their health suffer because they are slaves to a stressful job, or slaves to bad eating habits. This was the kind of grand vision that transcended self and family. It was a conscious, deliberate choice, and he proved himself willing to live true to that value.

This alone would have defined his legacy as a great and ethical warrior, but it was his actions after he was released from prison that earned him true reverence. One aspect of this was his commitment to reconciliation and non-racism and his actions in alignment with those values were represented in the movie *Invictus*. One scene showed his grandson making pejorative comments to two white policemen, at which Mandela senior reprimanded him. He was clear that being nonracist ran both ways and he acted on that principle. The movie also showed Mandela pressing forward with his commitment to support Springbok rugby and its right to maintain that name and emblem, despite both being seen as symbols of white dominance.

He met with strong opposition from within his own party for this and yet he persisted. From a unification point of view, it was a masterstroke. South African went on to win the 1995 Rugby World Cup and that achievement brought people together in a way that nobody could have anticipated.

The world is becoming an ever more complex place. There are ever more decisions to be made, more often, with fewer and fewer reference points—things like social or religious norms have been greatly diluted. Knowing your priority of values and living by them is one of the most important keys to surviving and being effective in this crazy new world.

4 | Your Power to Create

YOU HAVE a unique power as a human being to consciously direct the course of your life. You probably use it in some ways, like when you make a New Year's resolution, when you decide to chart a new course in your career, or when you pick yourself up after a relationship or business setback. Some people set out with great enthusiasm, but then don't follow through. Others persist, but have to use a lot of force or painful self-discipline. Either way, it can be exhausting, and you can get down on yourself.

In this chapter you'll learn exactly what power you're using when you set goals. You'll become better equipped to use that power to motivate yourself and stay motivated. You'll know what to do when you go off track, to get yourself back on track.

Chapter Theme Outcomes

Discover or learn more about the distinctive power you have as a human being, to have a say in creating your reality, using words.

By engaging in this chapter you will:

- ✓ Discover the unique power that you have as a human being that enables you to consciously create and direct the course of your life;
- ✓ Recognise the opportunities for you to use that power consciously and deliberately to pursue goals and transform your way of being;
- ✓ Learn how to use this power to motivate yourself and to maintain that level of motivation;
- ✓ Know what to do when you go off track, to get yourself quickly and effectively back on track.

 **KEY CONCEPT - TAKE NOTE**

Your Power to Create (Using Words)

THE POWER to decide and thereby to create is the power that separates human beings from all other life forms. We do this using language, or, more specifically, using words. Words give you the power to create.

Animals don't have words and so they cannot create, they can only react to their environment, and do what their instincts tell them to do. They don't design great cathedrals or machines like cranes to help them build. Humans can do those things, and more, and that power exists in our capacity to think and communicate consciously (and unconsciously!) using words.

When you make a decision, like a New Year's resolution, or when you chart a new course in your life or career, and even when you soothe yourself after a relationship breakup, or motivate yourself after a setback, you do all of that using words. First you think it, then you speak it, or write it down, and then, if you act on those words, it becomes a reality. For example, you say you'll get fit and run a marathon, or get a degree, or buy a house. Then, just like in the Kilimanjaro example in Chapter 1, you find out what you need to do; you do those things and, *voila*, you find yourself having that outcome—running the marathon, attending your graduation, or moving into your new house.

It's all so simple, right? Ha ha, not entirely, because you're not God. You can't say, "Let there be light," and there is light. For you and me, it works a little more slowly and less accurately. We have to struggle and work towards our goals; there are many obstacles, and sometimes we fall way short and have to try again. However, the principle is the same, and you are capable of tremendous feats of achievement as a result of your use of words.

The act of creation starts with what you might call a speech act. That means making a declaration, a statement of intent with commitment. This is usually demonstrated by using words like, "I will", "I promise", "I commit", "I am going to...", and so on. This is distinct from statements like, "I want to...", "I would like...", "I should...", "I need to...", etc. Those are merely expressions of an internal feeling state or idea and they generally don't lead to results.

One of the first things that people learn from coaching is to make this shift from expressing their plans as an idea or feeling state to expressing them in the form of a speech act. A speech act implies a commitment, which is why people shy away from it. So when you make this shift in language, you really feel its power—the power of the word.

The commitment implied by a speech act should be defined in space and time. In other words, what, by when. For example: I will run a marathon—by the end of summer; I will earn my bachelor's degree—in three years' time; I will buy a house—by the end of this year.

An important caveat to note here is that the commitment that is implied in a speech act is proven through action. So, making a speech act, and then demonstrating your commitment by action, is how you consciously bring anything into being. As Anthony Robbins has famously said, "I never leave the scene of a decision without taking one significant action."

You're not limited by what you can create using words.
And you do have to consider your domain of power.

Importantly, you're not limited by what you can create using words. You can create anything. John F. Kennedy made a speech act about putting a man on the moon and the Americans did it. So, yes, you can reach for the sky. And, at the same time, Kennedy was being realistic—in other words, he was stretching reasonably beyond the limits of his power—when he made that declaration. He knew that America had, or could at least develop, the capability to achieve that goal within the timeframe that he set. If a tribesman on a remote island had made the same speech act, well, it probably wouldn't have happened. It wouldn't have been realistic. So, while you're not limited by word, you do have to take into account your reality and consider your current domain of power and the resources that you have and can gain access to within the given timeframe.

Here are a number of things that arise as a result of making a speech act:

New thoughts, awareness and actions

You agree to climb Mt Kilimanjaro with a friend within six months. The next day, new thoughts occur: *What do I need? What will it cost?* Etc. For this reason, we always commit to the goal first, then think about how, and seldom, if ever, the other way around.

Attractor fields

Also consider the possibility that once something is created through a speech act, it takes on a life of its own; it becomes an "attractor field", and if you don't act on it to bring it about, somebody else will. Have you ever said you'd do something, but didn't, and then somebody else had that idea and did it?

Serendipity and flow

Many people have noticed how making a committed decision and then taking immediate action in alignment with that decision can also ignite favourable or supportive circumstances in alignment with the decision. There is a famous quote that supports this notion. It's often attributed to Goethe, however it seems to have originated from WH Murray, a mountain climber and Everest expedition leader. It goes like this: "Until one is committed there is hesitancy, the chance to draw back, always ineffectiveness. Concerning all acts of initiative and creativity there is one elementary truth, the ignorance of which kills countless ideas and splendid plans: that the moment one definitely commits oneself, then providence moves too. All sorts of things occur to help one that would never otherwise have occurred. A whole stream of events issues from the decision, raising in one's favour all manner of assistance, which no man could have dreamt would have come his way."

Now, if that doesn't inspire you to take on the challenge of using speech acts, then nothing will!

Being Your Word

Imagine a bungee jumper standing on the deck, ready to jump. She doesn't feel like it right then. She suddenly doesn't think it's a good idea. And she can still make the decision to jump. She can still act in alignment with her word. The principle that this example points to is this:

Your ability to act is independent of your thoughts and feelings.

Imagine these other scenarios:

- You make the commitment to go to gym tomorrow morning; you wake up and it's cold and raining and you don't feel like going...
- You decide to leave your job and start a new business and, on the way to hand in your resignation letter, you suddenly have doubts...
- You know that you should speak up in a meeting about an issue that concerns you, and you back down because of fear and self-doubt...

In all of these situations you can still act on your commitment. You can go to gym, hand in that letter, speak up, even though at the time you may not feel like it, or may have lost sight of the reasons why you thought it was a good idea in the first place.

It's possible, therefore, to do what you've committed to, even while your thoughts and feelings are momentarily not in alignment with that commitment. The truth is, they just haven't caught up with you yet!

Hopefully you can see the opportunity to use this principle to be a better person, a better citizen, better worker, leader, parent, and so on. You can use this principle to rise above your fears and prejudices and become the best version of yourself that you can be. All the power in the world lies in this little treasure vault!

Having Integrity with your Word

In scientific terms, when we say a system has integrity, we mean that it is whole, unified, or soundly constructed. For example, a bucket that has no leaks has integrity. Likewise, an electrical circuit. A system that lacks integrity—that has leaks in other words—will sooner or later lose all its contents: water in the case of a bucket; energy in the case of an electrical circuit. It only needs one small leak for the entire system to eventually run dry or stop working.

If you do everything that you say you're going to do, you'll start to believe in yourself.

In life, we human beings create our reality by speaking it into being—which can be called "giving a word" or "creating a word"—and then acting on that word. Integrity for the system that is a human being can therefore be defined as "doing what you say you will do". In other words, when you make a speech act, you create a container. As long as you're acting in alignment with that word, you maintain the integrity of that container. You literally feel your energy—your personal power, your self-belief, self-efficacy—build within that container.

Various benefits arise from being in integrity with your word. Firstly, if you say you're going to build a house by laying 100 bricks a day, and you do that, you will eventually get your house.

Secondly, if you do everything that you say you're going to do, then people—including you—will start to believe your speaking. They'll begin to trust you, and you'll start to trust yourself. You'll start to trust that what you say will become real. The more you do this, the higher your belief in your own self-efficacy becomes and the more energy you have for new commitments. It becomes a self-fulfilling prophecy.

Thirdly, acting in integrity with your word generates synchronicity and flow—or coincidences in your favour. This is based on the principle that you attract what you subconsciously believe, which is not just the domain of flaky New Agers, but also of credible psychologists like Carl Jung. So, if you believe that your own speaking will become real, because you have proved it many times, you maximise your potential to activate this principle. Or, to put it in more practical terms, consider Gary Player's famous maxim: "The more I practice, the luckier I get."

Recovering Integrity

What happens if you don't do what you said you would do? You break the circuit. You blow a hole in that container. In practical terms, you'll probably feel guilty. What's even more likely is that you'll lose energy around that commitment, or around your own self-efficacy. You may even give up on that goal entirely—and then perhaps on others as well. You may even punish yourself. None of these are constructive responses and they're all likely to lead into a downward spiral. If it involves a promise made to another person, they may lose trust in you. We can say that the system—who you say you are—has no integrity, and so it no longer holds energy.

So, if you find yourself breaking your word (i.e. not doing what you said you would do), whether it's a word to someone else or to yourself, the first thing you should do is to acknowledge—in other words, own up to—the fact, without beating yourself up. In fact, it's most appropriate to forgive yourself, with no justification needed. You just make a decision to forgive yourself. Then you can move to the next step. If it involves another person, then you could apologise or, even better, ask for their forgiveness, which gives them more power to respond honestly and appropriately.

Once you've cleared the air—whether it's with yourself or with another person—then re-commit to the goal and prove that commitment by taking immediate action. In other words, get back on the bicycle immediately.

To be complete, it would make sense to check with the other person, or with yourself, if there's anything you can do to make up for any possible loss that may have been incurred. This is not to be abused or to punish yourself. Just check. Perhaps you could go for a run right now, if it's to do with that goal of running a marathon and you missed a week of training. Or you could go right now and put out your kit so it's ready for tomorrow morning.

So, to summarise:

Step 1 Acknowledge the facts (that you didn't do what you said you would do) and face that as a simple fact.

Step 2 Choose to forgive yourself and let it go. Apologise, or ask for forgiveness, if it involves another person.

Step 3 Commit to get back on track immediately or as soon as possible. Prove that commitment by taking one significant action.

Step 4 Decide if you need to make amends.

Sometimes, you may recognise that a goal is not right for you. Be careful, however, that you're not just telling yourself that.

THE SCIENCE / THE SOURCE

Self-Creation using Word

THERE IS not much writing—and no research that I know of—that expands on the use and power of the word to create.

The most solid source I have found is in the book *The Four Agreements* by Don Miguel Ruiz. Ruiz is the current global spiritual head of the Toltec wisdom tradition, which stretches back thousands of years. In the aforementioned book, he presents four core agreements that, if kept, will lead to a harmonious life. The first agreement is given as: *Be impeccable with your word*. By this he means being careful what words you choose to describe or label yourself with—or any other person or situation.

He says, "Why your word? The word is the power that you have to create. The word is the gift that comes directly from God. The gospel of John in the Bible, speaking of the creation of the universe, says, 'In the beginning was the Word, and the Word was with God, and the word is God.' Through the word you express your creative power. It is through the word that you manifest every-thing. Regardless of what language you speak, your intent manifests through the word. What you dream, what you feel, and what you really are, will all be manifested through the word.

"The word is not just a sound or a written symbol. The word is a force; it is the power you have to express and communicate, to think, and thereby to create the events in your life. You can speak. What other animal on the planet can speak? The word is the most powerful tool you have as a human…"

The only other reference I've found is this one, and it refers to integrity, rather than to the word specifically, although one can understand integrity in this context to mean integrity to one's self-created word. It comes from the curriculum of the Maliwada Human Development Training School in Maliwada, India, which is a former program of The Institute of Cultural Affairs (ICA) International. It's quoted by Thea Westra on the Forward Steps blog and the full quote can be found at the following link: https://www.forwardstepsblog.com/2017/03/integrity/.

"We are going to visit the arena of profound humanness called 'Integrity'. Sometimes 'integrity' is reduced to mean a kind of moral uprightness and steadfastness, in the sense of saying, 'You have too much integrity to ever take a bribe.' Profound integrity goes far beyond this. Sometimes, in order to distinguish it from more limited popular usage, it is called 'secondary integrity'. This is the integrity which is not constrained by limited moralities, however well intentioned.

 "The integrity that is profound living is the singularity of thrust of a life committed and ordering every dimension of the self towards that commitment. Thus, the self is in fact shaped *by* the self, and focused towards that commitment. You can say that an audacious creation of the self takes place in integrity, without which you are simply the creation of the various forces impacting you in your society.

"Amid the flux of wavering to and fro that is so evident in others, you experience an inexplicable rootedness, as though you have sunk a taproot deep into the foundations of the earth itself. Though you experience life as a long journey, even an endless journey, towards the object of your resolve, yet you never sense yourself as a stranger on the journey. It's as if you'd been there before. Original integrity is experienced primarily by this sense of at-one-ness."

There are some deep truths in this theme of your power to create using words. Some, in particular, are expressed in the above *The Science / The Source* section. If you go into it, you might find that they are the deepest truths. In particular, the idea that a man creates himself—his or her *self*—by speaking it into being and then living in integrity with that self. That opens up a phenomenal possibility, if you think about it. It means you can apply the power to create using words to your inner state, or way of being, and not only to your external goals.

It means, for example, that instead of just waking up every day into whatever mood you find yourself in and then going through your day expressing every grumpy emotion and critical thought that arises, you can decide who to be. You can create a word to be a more inspiring leader, or parent, and then you can be that by acting in integrity with that word. You can become that person. You can retrain your brain.

It's a bit like being given a role in the end-of-year charity play, where you get told you're playing the bad guy, or Santa, or whatever. Your words and actions will arise out of your commitment to play that role. It works in just the same way that new thoughts arise out of a commitment to climb Kilimanjaro, except you're doing it with your personality, your way of being.

What do you do with your old thoughts and feelings, I hear you ask? You leave them behind. After all, you never created those, you just found yourself having them, so why be loyal to them? Sure, you can be honest about still having those thoughts and feelings, even while you're retraining your brain. You can admit those thoughts and feelings to yourself—and you should. You can admit them to others, or at least be willing to admit them if you're pressed to do so—that would be honest. Then you can take on your new way of being as a conscious intention and go out there and be that.

The more wholeheartedly you do it, the more people—including yourself—will buy it. After all, nobody wants to see a self-conscious actor. You want to see an actor who is immersed in their part.

So, if you're needing confidence, or to be a more inspirational person, speak it into being—say, "I am confident," or, "I am inspiring,"—and then act in integrity with your word to bring it about.

REAL-LIFE EXAMPLE

Being Precise About What You Want

AS A headstrong youth in my early twenties, I bought a car on auction—against my father's advice. He was right. It turned out to be a dud. Sadly, he passed away a few months later and then, only a week after that, the car was destroyed when a ten-ton truck ran a red light and smashed into me.

I decided to be smarter the next time about buying a car. I investigated financing options and calculated what would be the best car I could buy with the finance I could afford. I identified my target as being a white Citi Golf 1.6i 5-speed. And I wanted the one with black, instead of white, bumpers.

I wrote all this down and began the search. No luck on the first weekend, but on the second one, I stopped at a dealer and enquired. Nope, they had nothing that matched my requirements, the salesman said. As I was leaving, a car exactly matching my description pulled up and a father and daughter climbed out.

"You selling that car?" I asked them.

"Yes," the father said, "we're trading it in and we're here to collect her new car."

I signed the papers the same day and took delivery a week later.

I didn't know it at the time, but I was exercising the principle of the power of the word.

Something similar happened a few years later, after my now ex-wife and I had moved to Cape Town with our son. We were living in Fresnaye, which was too hot and noisy for my liking and gave off a terrible glare from the ocean every afternoon. I proposed a move to the back of the mountain, to the cool shade of Newlands. Fortunately, she agreed.

We wrote down the details of the house we wanted. In Fresnaye we had a place with too many levels and most of the space went unused. We decided a small cabin-like space would suit us better, one where all the rooms centred on the main living space. Oh, and it should have a skylight with a view of the mountain, a swimming pool, and we'd want there to be blinds already installed instead of having to do that ourselves.

With the list written and filed, we began the search. It was only three weeks later that I received a call from an agent. He had a house he thought I should look at, and described it to me. It sounded perfect. What's more, I happened to be just down the road from the address he gave.

I drove directly to the place; he met me there and showed me around. It matched every single item we'd specified. We signed an offer that same afternoon.

Of course, things like this don't happen all the time. Sometimes there seems to be a "rightness" to what you specify and then things just work out—they really do manifest exactly according to your specifications.

Perhaps we need to learn to listen better to what's out there, to what's needed by the whole situation instead of just what we want in order to defend against our fears. Perhaps, when we do that, then we get it right. I certainly don't want to encourage flaky beliefs or superstitions. After all, this is not an area that science has addressed. In fact, it's not an area that the religions have addressed much either. Perhaps you'll find it in the Jewish Kabbala, and in the field of ontology, which is the study of the nature of being and which is a major influence in the practice of coaching, particularly as I learned to practice it. Therefore, you're invited to try it on and test it for yourself and share with others what you discover.

5 | Decision & Commitment

ARE YOU the kind of person who just drifts along and lets life happen? Or, when you know you need to do something, do you take a long time to convince yourself? Then, are you easily distracted? Or are you someone who makes clear decisions and commitments even before you know how you're going to achieve that goal. Do you keep yourself on track when you've made a commitment?

In this chapter, you'll discover the importance of consistently making clear decisions and the power that a commitment has to shift your mental state and your level of energy in any situation. You'll also see how commitments spark new ideas and solutions that you would never have had otherwise.

Chapter Theme Outcomes

Discover or learn more about the importance of decisions and the power of making firm, clear commitments.

By engaging in this chapter you will:

- ✓ Discover the need for, and the secret to, quick, easy, clear decision-making;
- ✓ Recognise where you might be lacking clarity and what you can do about it;
- ✓ Learn what you can put in place so that you can make quick, clear decisions in every situation;
- ✓ Know how to organise your life according to what's most important to you and what you're best at.

KEY CONCEPT - TAKE NOTE

Decision & Commitment

A DECISION is a mental action that leads to the elimination of one option—or range of options—for the sake of another. In fact, the Latin root of the word decision is most telling: *decidere*, meaning "to cut off". If you look at it, every decision—even a win-win decision—always involves a cutting off of one path, or course of action, over another. To be with one person, you're asked to eliminate being with others. To pursue a career in one field, you have to forego others. To own a Windows PC, you have to walk away from a Mac. Sheesh, this is difficult stuff!

In addition, decisions are forced on you by the movement of life. You get to a certain age and you have to decide on a career. You get to the end of your contract and you have to decide whether to renew it. The important point to note here is that life keeps moving, and it gives you a brief window to have your say. You can take that opportunity or not. The train is going to leave the station and you can get on that train, or not.

In fact, as Napoleon Hill, author of one of the earliest and best self-help books, *Think & Grow Rich*, wrote, "Life is a draughts board, and the player opposite you is time. If you hesitate before moving, or neglect to move promptly, your draughts will be wiped off the board by time. You are playing against a partner who will not tolerate indecision!"

No wonder that the world-famous life coach Anthony Robbins places so much emphasis on the importance and power of decisions. "It is in the moments of decision that your destiny is shaped," he says.

Right there sits the clue as to why you may sometimes struggle to make decisions. The ego, you saw in Chapter 2, starts out as a defence mechanism. It gets set up, to a large degree, as a strategy for avoiding what you don't like. This continues into adult life, where your ego still tries to either control, or resist, any movement or change in a direction that it doesn't like.

You're likely to demonstrate this control or resistance by either leaping forward impulsively with decisions, in an attempt to control the situation very tightly, or, at the other end of the spectrum, by avoiding the decision entirely. Either way, those are indicators that the ego is trying to prevent the changes that it doesn't want.

Decisions are necessary, as we saw, to keep pace with life, and life doesn't really stand around waiting to find out what you want. Therefore, it's not about getting those decisions "right" so much as it is about making them fast enough that you don't get left behind. Therefore, you're better off being like that sportsperson on the field, who knows that any decision is better than no decision. This was certainly the view of Theodore Roosevelt, who said, "In any moment of decision, the best thing you can do is the right thing, the next best thing is the wrong thing, and the worst thing you can do is nothing."

Of course, a deliberate decision to *not* act, or to leave a situation to take its own course, is still a decision, which is different from doing nothing in the sense of just ignoring it and hoping it will go away. It's about making decisions and being willing to deal with the consequences. The more you can do this, the more you'll reduce stress and improve your experience of life.

THE SCIENCE / THE SOURCE

The Role of Emotions in Decisions

EMOTIONS HAVE received a bad rap when it comes to decision-making. They've been seen as interfering to the point that, in business, it's often said that you need to "keep emotions out of the decision". Women, in particular, have borne the brunt of this prejudice. Yet, a number of studies have shown that emotions are essential to good decision-making—and that you use them in ways that you don't even realise.

Back in the 1950s, the prefrontal lobotomy was a widely used "treatment" for people who had been diagnosed as schizophrenic, or who had severe OCD or depression. Essentially, it involved severing the fibres that connected the prefrontal cortex to the rest of the brain.

The prefrontal cortex is the area recognised for, inter alia, complex cognitive behaviour, decision-making and social behaviour. Yet these operations removed, not only intellectual capacity, but also emotional capacity. This served as an early clue that emotions and decision-making were bound up.

Many years later, one of the world's leading neuroscientists, Dr Antonio Damasio, made a similar finding with one of his patients, a successful businessman whom he named Elliott. Elliott had suffered brain damage as a result of a tumour and subsequent surgery for removal. According to Damasio, "Elliott emerged as a man with a normal intellect who was unable to decide properly, especially when the decision involved personal or social matters." Apparently, it took Elliott 30 minutes to choose an appointment time, and even longer to decide where to have lunch, and he even struggled to decide what colour pen to use to fill out office forms. All this despite the fact that he remained in the 97th percentile in terms of his IQ score.

Damasio provided Elliott as a case study in his 1994 book, *Descarte's Error*, in which, according to the Amazon blurb, Damasio "challenged traditional ideas about the connection between emotions and rationality" and proffered that "emotions are not a luxury, they are essential to rational thinking and to normal social behaviour". In fact, far from excluding them, we can't do without them, he insists.

The orbitofrontal cortex is a region within the prefrontal cortex of the brain which is involved in the cognitive processing of decision-making. The amygdala, we know, is the seat of our most primitive reactions, in particular our fight-or-flight response, and therefore the wellspring of our emotions. Damasio's somatic marker hypothesis describes the interplay between the two. It has the amygdala and the orbitofrontal cortex being intricately linked to form a neural circuit critical for judgment and decision-making.

"Nature appears to have built the apparatus of rationality (the orbitofrontal cortex) not just on top of the apparatus of biological regulation (the amygdala), but also from it and with it," he wrote in *Descarte's Error*.

This statement implies that emotions provide additional information, for example in the form of motivation and meaning, to rational factors when making decisions. Without it, for starters, we'd get stuck in analysis paralysis. Then, as the author of *How We Decide*, Jonah Lehrer, points out, "Emotion and motivation share the same Latin root, *movere*, which means to move. The world is full of things and it is our feelings that help us choose [and therefore move] among them."

Lehrer postulates that our best decisions are a finely tuned blend of both feeling and reason—and the precise mix depends on the situation. He states that "Emotions are profoundly smart and constantly learning, they are not simply animal instincts that must be tamed."

So, what goes into making a good decision? Well, the first thing to recognise is that when you're facing a decision, you're effectively attempting to answer a question. Usually, that question is something like, *How can I get what I want?* This usually points you back to your values, which, remember, you're committed to more than anything, to the point that you're willing to die for them—assuming that you're human and just like everybody else.

This is the one reason why we tend to make the same decision again and again throughout our lives, each time with different content. Think about that guy who misses his child's birthday, not once, but again and again. Although the content of the situation appears different each time, in effect, he's just demonstrating—unconsciously, without awareness—his commitment to his priority of values.

> *When you're facing a decision, you're effectively attempting to answer a question.*

Or, another question that you might effectively be trying to answer when facing a decision goes like this: *How can I make sure that the thing I fear most doesn't happen?* Remember that enneagram avoidance area, that red zone trigger? Well, presuming again that you're human and much like everybody else, then you're likely to be just as committed to avoiding that thing as you are to living out your priority of values. No wonder, then that you can often find yourself getting stuck, or getting into conflict with other people, with regards to a decision because you're trying to control or resist a particular outcome.

In the *Practical Mindfulness* program we show that you're not so much in charge of every situation as you are a part of the situation—and that you're far less able to direct the situation than you would like to believe. Therefore, if your question is all about you and what you want, it's likely to be out of sync with the reality of the situation, or the reality of life. It's a harsh truth that's coming up here, but life doesn't always care too much about what you want. It's not a giant ATM waiting for you to come and type in your PIN code and make your withdrawal.

Therefore, a better question that you can use to guide your decision-making would be one that takes the reality of life into account—the reality that you're part of the bigger picture, you're part of what wants to happen in the situation. So that would be a better question then, wouldn't it? Asking, *What wants to happen in this situation? Or, What might happen in this situation that might turn out OK, even if it's not what I want?* Then you might ask, *What's my part in that? Or, What do I need to do?*

If those questions don't entirely work for you, the principle still stands. When you're making a decision, you're effectively asking a question. If you can identify what question you're asking and then address whether that's the best question to be asking in the situation, you'll be taking the essential step towards better decision-making. The next step would be to determine what would be the best question to be asking and addressing, preferably one that doesn't assume that you're the master of the universe, because that's not realistic, no matter how much you've developed the power of your word!

REAL-LIFE EXAMPLE

Vasbyt!—The Mother of All Challenges

I SERVED my mandatory national service in the South African military during the late 1980s. On the officers' course, you knew that one day you would be woken up for the endurance hike that was commonly known as *Vasbyt*.

Vasbyt is an Afrikaans word that translates to "bite the bullet" and it's a perfect moniker for this activity, which is an adventure race on steroids in which the training officers do their very best to break you psychologically.

To kick it off, they woke us with sirens in the middle of the night. They allocated equipment for us to carry, but insufficient materials to make the braces we needed to carry it on. Even so, we had to lug this equipment along a narrow crevice of space that ran between a steep embankment and a railway line. For miles. For hours. For a whole day, it turned out.

Towards sunset, we were allowed to drop our load and we marched on easier terrain. Up ahead was a luxurious-looking tent. Ah, this would not be so bad, we all thought. We were directed past the tent, down the road and into the night.

All through the night we were given scouting exercises to do. If you returned without the right information, you were sent back. It was freezing cold, so that if you sat still for too long you froze. All the while, officers drove along the route in trucks offering you a ride back to camp if you wanted to give up. Many did.

The next day things got tougher, and more pointless, and the encouragement was still there for you to give up and hop on a truck and go home. Today, thirty years later, I still remember clearly the moment on that second day when I decided that I would not give up. I would finish this. I would own it. I would conquer it. I would make it my own.

At that moment I felt a surge of energy flood through me. I felt alive and powerful in a way that I had never known.

By day three I had no food left. By day four, it was each to his own and you had to find your way home, before cut-off time. For the last half a day we walked back along that railway line. Everyone was too exhausted and hungry to even speak. You just put one foot in front of the other and dared not stop.

I just made the cut-off time and, soon after, I found myself back in my bungalow. I felt reluctant to remove my backpack. *Is that all?* I thought. *That wasn't so bad! I could go again!* I felt that I could do more. The four days seemed to have flown by.

Before the army, I had always enjoyed running for fitness. I had run a distance of five to eight kilometres, almost daily, throughout my teenage years. When I returned home after having completed *Vasbyt*, I noticed that my running times dropped by a quarter.

The reason? I had always paced myself and kept something in reserve. After *Vasbyt*, I knew that it was all in the mind, that you could push yourself so much harder and that, when you did, you entered the zone, that place where nothing mattered, where pain was pleasure, and you could go forever—and all because of a decision to totally own an apparently impossible activity!

Think about times when you've made a decision. Perhaps it was to resign from your lousy job or to finally leave a destructive relationship. Or to start a new business, or a new relationship. There's a tremendous amount of energy that comes with any decision, as illustrated in the previous, real-life example. It's easy, then, to take action at the point of decision. In fact, the energy compels you to. Very often, you get a positive response from life. Some big coincidence happens that seems to confirm your decision. It's like you're being given some big reward from the universe for finally taking action.

More than anything, decisions require courage.
You need to embrace the movement of life.

The challenge, then, is to sustain that energy and continue with that commitment, with taking action in that direction. You can quickly develop doubts, like that good old buyer's remorse. It's realistic to pay attention to that, and more often than not, it's the old ego defence mechanism, that old self, that small self that held you in that place for so long, that's having one last-gasp attempt to survive by getting you back. Be careful, when you've made a decision, to refer back to the principle of integrity and being your word. Stay with the decision, stay with the commitment, despite what those niggly doubts may tell you—and you can be sure they'll know exactly what arguments to throw at you!

You can probably see that, more than anything, decisions require courage. They also result in movement and the elimination of options. So, apart from asking yourself better questions, you need to embrace the movement of life and see that things often turn out OK, or even better than you'd hoped. This will give you the courage you need and the willingness to move with life. In fact, you'd be well advised to gather some evidence from your past when that was the case.

Secondly, you need to have—or to develop—the willingness to let go of options, to cut your losses, to take one single path and find the riches that become available by taking that path, that would not have become available if you'd tried to keep your options open. Once again, gather some evidence from your life of when eliminating a range of options for the sake of one particular option resulted in a positive outcome, whether it was in terms of knowledge, experience, love, career, money, or some other factor.

Here's one more thing to know about decisions. When you get up on a weekday morning, and you have to get the kids to school and yourself to work, there's not much debating to do, is there? Your priorities and decisions are handed to you by the very clear and tight deadlines you have, and to which you are most definitely committed. Conversely, when you wake up on a Sunday morning and there are no plans, you can debate endlessly about what to do, and when. The difference? There is no commitment to any particular activity or outcome, and no deadlines.

The thing to see here is the link between having a tightly defined context and decision-making. The more clear your context is, the more the decisions just present themselves, there's no debate needed. On weekdays, your context for decision-making is provided by the "clear and tight deadlines" and the loop is closed by your commitment to those deadlines. On weekends, there's no such thing and so you lay around, slow to decide anything.

Naturally, this brings us back, once more, to the Kilimanjaro example. You gave yourself a clear context (climb Kilimanjaro) and a tight deadline (six months), and made a firm commitment to that deadline. Suddenly, you knew exactly what to do, evidenced by the new thoughts that arose the next day.

So, what does this mean? It means be as busy as you can. Ha ha, that's a joke. It means that you should always know where you're going. Begin with the end in mind. Have a clear goal or outcome or intention. Then commit to a deadline. You'll find that most of your decisions will make themselves.

We'll revisit this subject on a much bigger scale in Chapter 12, the final chapter, when you create your *Legacy & Lifestyle Statement*. For now, before you leave this page, what decision do you choose to make?!

6 | Story & Reality

HAVE YOU ever tried to change someone's mind about something, only to hear them come up with reasons why they should keep doing things their way, even though they've not been producing results? When people do that, they seem convinced by their own arguments, don't they?

Have you ever noticed that if you ask ten people about a situation, you'll get ten points of view? Yet everybody's convinced that their own version of things—their own *story*—perfectly describes the *reality*, aren't they?

Have you ever gone outside and told the weather how upset you are about it being grey on the day? Has the reality of the weather ever changed because of your story about the weather? No!

In this chapter you'll learn a distinction between reality (what *happens*) and your narrative, or story, *about* what happens. You'll learn to deal with what's real and what matters in order to produce results.

Chapter Theme Outcomes

This chapter will introduce the distinction between what happens and your narrative—or story—*about* what happens. You'll learn to recognise when you're "in story" and make the shift to "deal with what's real".

By engaging in this chapter you will:

- ✓ Discover the difference between what's real and what's not real in any situation, and what does and doesn't matter for producing results;
- ✓ Recognise when you're losing presence and going "into story";
- ✓ Learn to spot different types of story;
- ✓ Know what you can do to stay in touch with what's real and what matters—especially when it matters.

KEY CONCEPT - TAKE NOTE

Story & Reality

WHEN YOU learn to meditate, you often begin by training yourself to put your attention on your breath. You notice very quickly that your mind wanders and that keeping your attention on the facts, the data—in this case your breath—is not easy to do. If you pay attention, you'll notice that where your mind wanders to is your thoughts and imagination. For example, you'll very quickly find yourself playing out a scenario that happened—or that you'd like to have happen—at work or with your partner. Even if you become quite good at it and keep your attention on your breath for a while, the slightest disturbance can set it off. The sound of a dog barking, a cold breeze on your skin, or even nothing—the thoughts will just come. Whatever the disturbance, your imagination is very quickly activated.

That example is emblematic of what happens and how your mind behaves in your life in general. If you observe carefully, you'll see that while you're driving or when you're sitting in meetings, you're often distracted by your own thoughts. And what's going on inside your mind? Your interpretation of things. I like this. I don't like that. I agree with this. I disagree with that. I think this. I think that. I wonder what's going on with the cricket? Why's she wearing that colour, it doesn't suit her? And so on.

And then, just let somebody mention your name, and you'll be fully present and alert and paying attention. But just let them say something about you that you don't like or agree with, and what will you do? You'll pull out your story. *Your* version of events. Even if you've been presented with a set of facts, or data, you'll still want to give it your spin, your story. Or let's say you haven't done what you said you would do. That's usually quite a hard fact. Here comes your story.

So we can say that we invest a great amount of time and energy in our story. Much more than we do in the facts and, therefore, much more than we do in reality. We can also say that things happen (or don't happen!) in reality and the mind is a mechanism that attaches meaning (explanations, justifications, STORY) to the things that happen (or don't happen). These explanations seldom have anything to do with the reality of what happened and even less often do they make a difference to what happened, or to what needs to happen. Your story doesn't make a difference to the fact.

Here are some more examples:

1. Someone is late, and they give you the story, all the reasons why. Does it make a difference? No! Rather deal with the fact—*I am late!*—and complete using the procedure for recovering integrity.
2. You said you were going to go to gym / finish that report / start your own business, but you didn't. What do you do? You justify it with all the reasons why (your story). While you're telling your story, does the job get done? No.
3. You have a flat tyre and you're on the phone complaining about tyre manufacturers or people who throw glass on the road. Does it get the problem solved? No. You need to change the tyre.

So you can see that story and reality—the facts, the data, "what is"—are two different operating realms, and that you're either in one or in the other. You can't be in both at the same time. Yet, if you want to impact reality, you have to act in the realm where reality is. So the purpose of this distinction is to increase your power to impact reality.

The problem is when you think reality will shift in response to your story. It doesn't—and it won't.

There's nothing wrong with story when you use it correctly, for example, to find out what happened in order to improve performance, or to entertain. The problem arises, firstly, when you believe that reality will shift in response to your story. Reality does not shift for your story. Secondly, when you believe that your story is the real "reason" or "meaning" for why something happened or didn't happen. For example, that not getting the deal means, "I'm a failure," or, "It wasn't meant to be." You can be sure that your "reason" or "meaning" is just your interpretation. Ask someone else, they will see it differently—they'll offer their interpretation. The situation is what it is; the "meaning" or interpretation is interesting, perhaps useful in some cases, but certainly not the absolute truth.

Opinions are story, and opinions don't make a difference to the reality out there. Action does! If it's making a difference you're after, the more powerful response is, "What am I going to do about it?" or, "What will I do differently the next time?" or, "How can I make this happen?"

Statements such as, "I want...", "I need...", "I should..." are all in the realm of story. Speech acts such as, "I will...", "I commit...", "I promise...", "I am going to...", and the actions that follow them, are in the realm of reality, and will produce results.

We can say, then, that there are two kinds of people in the world, those who have what they want, and those who have the reasons (the story) why not.

In language, you'll find that everything after "but" and "because" in a sentence, and everything that answers the question, "Why?" is a story—as explanation, justification, rationalisation. This is the reason why the questions beginning with the word, ,"Why?" are never asked in coaching Psychotherapy, on the other hand, is all about asking why, and so no wonder it takes you into years of useless story.

As you can see, there is no power derived from living in story.

THE SCIENCE / THE SOURCE

Cognitive Distortions

COGNITIVE DISTORTIONS are particular forms of story that run in our minds. They get reinforced by an internal narrative that seems rational, but which in fact arises out of that same faulty thinking and is therefore self-justifying, as story always is.

The psychologist Aaron Beck first proposed the theory behind cognitive distortions in 1976. It was popularised in the 1980s by David Burns. Below are some common cognitive distortions

Filtering Taking the negative details and magnifying those while filtering out all positive aspects of a situation. For example, picking out a single, unpleasant detail and dwelling on it exclusively so that your vision of reality becomes distorted.

Polarized (or "Black and White") Thinking Seeing things as either black-or-white, all-or-nothing. For example, you have to be perfect or you're a complete and abject failure— there is no middle ground.

Overgeneralization Coming to a general conclusion based on a single incident or single piece of evidence. For example, a student gets a poor grade on one paper in one semester, then concludes they are a horrible student and should quit school.

Jumping to Conclusions Claiming to know what another person is feeling or thinking, or why they act the way they do. For example, a person may conclude that someone is holding a grudge against them, but doesn't actually bother to find out if it's true.

Personalization Believing that everything others do or say is some kind of direct, personal reaction to you. For example, "We were late to the dinner party and caused everyone to have a terrible time. I should have pushed to leave on time."

Fallacy of Control Believing that you—or some other external force, or person—is in complete control of every situation in your life. This results in either personalising as above, or blaming—seeing yourself as a victim of fate.

Fallacy of Fairness Feeling resentful because you think you know what's fair, but other people—or life—won't agree with you. It continues being unfair!

Fallacy of Change Believing that you can get someone else to change to suit you if you just pressure or cajole them enough—and that they need to make that change for you to be happy. For example, a girlfriend who tries to get her boyfriend to change "just a few minor things".

Shoulds Having ironclad rules about how things should be or how people—including yourself—should behave, then getting angry when they don't; or feeling guilty when *you* don't.

Always Being Right Putting other people on trial to prove that your own opinions and actions are the absolute correct ones.

—adapted from: John M. Grohol, Psy.D., 15 Common Cognitive Distortions, *Psych Central*, Last updated: 17 Jan 2019; https://psychcentral.com/lib/15-common-cognitive-distortions/

You gain power when you become aware of your story *as story*, especially the story that you tell yourself consistently about who you are, and why things are the way they are. You'd call this your "personal narrative", or your "internal narrative". It consists of all the reasons why you can't have the things you want. The reasons why you keep failing at this or that. The reasons why you don't deserve this or that. You could look to shift that into a more realistic, perhaps more positive, narrative.

Now there's no need to go into psychotherapy to find out why you think those things. That can often just take you deeper into story and perpetuate the problem. The best way to shift your internal narrative is to create a word and act on that word, without story. In other words, set yourself a goal, make decisions and take action towards that goal. Then measure the results and record the facts. See how getting out of story produces results. You'll very quickly build a positive narrative, one that will be based on evidence. Just a caution: if you're a so-called optimist with a permanently positive narrative, be careful that it's not just a way of denying the facts or avoiding reality. You may need to get out of that story in order to do what's needed and move things forward.

REAL-LIFE EXAMPLE

The Endless Search for Meaning

I WENT through a time in my life when I became obsessed with finding meaning. I wanted a conclusive, definitive statement, something I could put on a plaque on the wall and say, "That's it!" Perhaps I thought it would solve all the world's problems—and make me rich and famous at the same time if I could write it up into a book!

I spent a lot of time ruminating and thinking and found it hard to focus on work. My attention kept getting pulled to this problem. Yet, the more I thought about it, the more meaningless everything seemed, and the things I wanted to do in the world seemed ever more enormous, ever further away.

Naturally, I became quite unproductive and this set up a cycle of negative reinforcement. My response was to search deeper still. It was as if I believed I could think my way out of the problem and, by thinking about it, land up at a perfect understanding of life.

I recognise now that I unconsciously expected that once I achieved that understanding, life would deliver some miracle outcome that I could live into. If not a literal winning of the lottery then some other version of that—the ultimate job, or public recognition and acceptance for my writing on a grand scale, whatever it turned out to be.

I reached a point of crisis before I saw that thoughts without action did not produce results. I saw that I could choose to put my attention on work and productive outputs, even though they seemed mundane and even though holding my attention there—and not drifting off into the search for meaning—was probably the most difficult challenge I had ever encountered.

I generally felt better once I'd completed a task, and over time I learned to trust that, if I remained productive, the thoughts that called me like a siren's voice towards the search for meaning would eventually dissolve and disappear without me having to engage them. I developed to the point where, no matter how much that thinking called me, I could switch smoothly and easily into action—doing the next most important task that would take me towards my main goal, a goal that I learned not to question, but just to keep on moving towards.

Note that this is not to say that one should never think, nor should it be used to justify impulsive action. Using thinking, instead of letting thinking and analysing get out of control, is the desired goal.

A good way to get yourself, or anybody else out of story, is by asking them either an out-of-the-box, or a practical, question, one that gets them to look at the facts of the situation, or that simply stops their thinking in its tracks. You don't even wait for them to finish a sentence, you just ask it while they're speaking. My favourite is, "So, what's true for you right now?"
It gets them every time.

7 | Taking Responsibility

THERE'S THAT classic joke where the guy asks the woman, "What's wrong?" and she says, "Nothing." Of course, it's not nothing, but she won't tell him; he has to guess. We often find ourselves on one or the other side of that equation. Sometimes you don't know what the other person wants, and they won't ask. Or, you're the one sulking or feeling frustrated and you don't even realise it—or know why.

In this chapter you'll learn how to instantly shift yourself from a state of frustration (and other disempowered states) to a state of positive responsibility and action. You'll discover that you can always ask for what you want—as long as you're willing to live with the answer that you get.

Chapter Theme Outcomes

Discover or learn more about the main cause of frustration, what the links are between that and responsibility—and what you can do about it.

By engaging in this chapter you will:

- ✓ Discover the main cause of frustration and what to do about it;
- ✓ Recognise where you are on the path to frustration with regards to any issue;
- ✓ Learn how to instantly shift yourself from a state of frustration (and other disempowered states) to a state of positive responsibility and action;
- ✓ Know how you can always ask for what you want—as long as you're willing to live with the answer that you get.

Taking Responsibility

AT LEAST a dozen or more times a day, something happens—or doesn't happen—and you develop a preference: a wish, will or desire. It comes up as a thought in your mind, or as a feeling, an energy. For example, you realise you've had enough, you now want to be paid more for what you do; or you decide you want more public recognition from your boss for your creative input; or you would like flowers from your husband occasionally, or for your wife to make you a sandwich once in a while.

Often, you don't communicate your wish, will or desire. Perhaps you're too shy, or you're playing a political game. Or you simply think you shouldn't have to—the other person should know. Or you think everyone should approach life in the way that you do, want what you want and, in addition, give you what you want. Instead, you send out signals, for example by withholding your energy or participation—or, in other words, sulking.

When you do that, you're sliding downwards into the state of victimhood and avoiding responsibility. Why? Well, if you think about it, it's OK for a baby to expect that its mother should intuit what it wants. After all, it can't talk, and it doesn't know what the options are. You, on the other hand, are a grown-up. You know what you want—or you can figure it out, at least—and you're responsible for getting it. How do you do that? Well, how else, but by asking for it?

Tool: The Ladder of Power

The tool that you'll be introduced to in this chapter is called the *Ladder of Power*. It's a powerful tool that should be your first check whenever you're unhappy with a situation or any of your relationships is not working. This version is adapted from the original, which was developed by Marc Steinberg, founder of the Consciousness Coaching Academy. It goes like this:

Expectation

An expectation is an uncommunicated wish, will or desire. In any relationship, whether work or personal, you'll "expect" people to show up in a certain way, perhaps because, you tell yourself, "That's how friends are", or "He's a guy, he should know," etc. Of course, the other person doesn't

Tool: The Ladder of Power

Study this tool to identify where and how you can take greater responsibility.

Make a request	Response required (yes/no); agreement created	**The Key** When asking, allow the other person to say, "No."
Express a wish	Just putting it on the table; no response needed	
Preference	"I need…" / "I would like…"	When you get a "No" answer, ask yourself: Is this a need (core value that I choose not to live without) or is it a want (something I can live without)?
Expectation	Sighing, sulking; "the look"; thinking they should know	
Complaint	Talking to others, but not to the person involved	**Note** The slide downwards is progressive: you will go through each stage until you reach the bottom. The step upwards is instant and direct —you may go to straight to the request without having to express a wish first.
Frustration	"I'm so frustrated." Indirect (passive) aggression.	
Resignation	"I give up." "That's just how he is / she is / the company is / the world is."	

Source: Marc Steinberg,
Consciousness Coaching® Academy

know. Perhaps they haven't noticed, or their idea of friendship or of being a guy doesn't involve doing that thing.

Complaint

An unmet expectation will inevitably devolve to a complaint. A complaint is indicated by the fact that you're telling someone other than the person concerned. You complain to your spouse about your work colleague, to your friend about your spouse, and so on. Naturally, this never produces a result and so you'll inevitably slide down to the next level.

Frustration

Frustration is most commonly indicated by the use of the phrase, "I'm frustrated." If you hear or think that phrase, you most likely have an unexpressed wish, will or desire that you've complained about and which has devolved to this stage. Frustration can often be expressed in a passive aggressive manner, or through indirect anger: you kick the photocopy machine when, really, you're frustrated with your boss, and so on.

Resignation

Resignation in this context means giving up. It means you've told yourself you've tried everything and it's no good. If you find out the things people are most resigned about, then, often, you'll find the things they're most passionate about. The problem is that they haven't found a way to ask for those things, or have not accepted the answer that they're getting.

The downward slide along the Ladder of Power is both progressive and inevitable. You'll go through all the stages and you'll end up at the bottom, on any issue that you don't communicate.

The jump to the top half of the ladder is theoretically simple, although in practice in can cause major sweats and require a serious commitment to do.

Express a wish

This means you're just putting it on the table. You're telling the other person what the issue is. It doesn't require a yes or no response from them, and it doesn't lead to any agreements. If you've ever done this, you'll know that it leads to a great amount of relief and, possibly, a great release of energy.

You'd do this by saying something like, "My wish is that you'd [wash your hands before you eat]." Or, "I'd really like it if you…" and so on.

Make a request

This step involves making a formal request that requires a yes/no response and therefore inevitably leads to an agreement. You'd express this by saying something like, "I request that you..." or, "Would you please..." or, "I ask that you..." and so on. This may sound formal and that's OK. It may be that you're not used to asking for what you want. And it may be that it needs to be stated formally. You may find ways to state it less formally. Either way, you might also end your statement with the phrase, "Do you agree, yes or no?"

It's important to walk away with an actual agreement—or a clear *no*. If you get a yes, then great, you can move on, and you'll have to monitor whether they actually go through with it or not and hold them accountable. If you get a no, or an effective no because they said yes but they never meant it and so they never act on it, then you have a choice. Is this a non-negotiable need that you're not prepared to compromise on? If so, then you have to make a tough choice. If it's something you'd like, but you can live without, well, then you've done what you can, and you can make your adjustments around that. You may even decide to wait awhile and ask again.

> *It's important to walk away with an actual agreement—or a clear no.*

Of course, genuine asking means giving the other person permission to say no. Otherwise you're pretending to ask, but you're really just trying to force them to do or to give you what you want. That's disingenuous. It also puts you back into the loop with an expectation—the expectation that the other person should say yes—and that's when you'll deceive yourself that you're doing all you can by asking and asking and yet you're still frustrated. The key to the "power" in the Ladder of Power is that you are willing and ready to accept whatever answer you get and then act accordingly, even if it means you have to end the particular form of the relationship.

This last point is the primary reason why we don't act in this way. We'd rather try to force, manipulate or cajole the other person than take responsibility for what we want and face up to the truth about what that means for our relationships.

On the next page is an exercise to get you started with using the Ladder of Power. You'll identify where you are and what you plan to do about it.

PRACTICAL EXERCISE — DO THIS NOW

The Ladder of Power

USE THIS tool to identify what issues you need to take responsibility for and what actions you'll take, and by when.

Instructions	Instructions
Instructions **Step 1** Identify the issue that's currently occupying your time, energy and attention and which you're either thinking about, complaining about, frustrated about, or which you've completely given up on.	**Step 2** Choose the relevant conversion action (i.e. expressing a wish or making a request) that you'll take, who you'll address it to, and by when you'll have done that.
EXAMPLE	**EXAMPLE**
An **expectation** I'm currently carrying around with me is:	The conversion **action** I will take is:
The fact that my deadlines keep changing and nobody ever asks if it's OK with me. People should ask me first if it's OK with me.	By Friday this week I will make a request to my boss that I should be consulted before any decisions are made regarding deadlines that affect me.
Expectations	**Expectations**
An **expectation** I'm currently carrying around with me is:	The **action** I will take is:
	By [DATE] I will express a wish / make a request to [person] that he / she / they:

Complaints		Complaints		Complaints
Something I'm currently **complaining** about is:		The **action** I will take is:		
	⇨	By [DATE] I will express a wish / make a request to [person] that he / she / they:		

Frustrations		Frustrations		Frustrations
Something I'm currently **frustrated** about is:		The **action** I will take is:		
	⇨	By [DATE] I will express a wish / make a request to [person] that he / she / they:		

Resigned / Given Up		Resigned / Given Up		
Something I'm resigned to / have given up on is:		The **action** I will take is:		
	⇨	By [DATE] I will express a wish / make a request to [person] that he / she / they:		

The Real Meaning of "I Do"

WHEN AN infant [is hungry, or its diapers are wet] it signals distress the only way it knows how—with an undifferentiated cry—and if its caretakers are perceptive enough, the infant is fed, changed, held, or rocked, and experiences momentary satisfaction. But if [that doesn't happen], the child experiences a primitive anxiety: the world is not a safe place. Since it has no way of taking care of itself and no sense of delayed gratification, it believes that getting the outside world to respond instantly to its needs is truly a matter of life and death.

Although you and I have no recollection of these first few months of life, our old brains are still trapped in an infantile perspective. Although we are now adults, capable of keeping ourselves fed and warm and dry, a hidden part of us still expects the outside world to take care of us. [This] plays a key role in marriage.

[For] most couples there is a noticeable change in the relationship about the time they make a definite commitment to each other. Once they say, "Let's get married," or, "Let's get engaged," [...] the pleasing, inviting dance of courtship draws to a close, and lovers begin to want not only the expectation of need fulfilment [...] but the reality as well. Suddenly it isn't enough that their partners be affectionate, clever, attractive, and fun-loving. They now have to satisfy a whole hierarchy of expectations, some conscious, but most hidden from their awareness. [...]

For example, a man may expect his new bride to do the housework, cook the meals, shop for groceries, wash the clothes, arrange the social events, take on the role of family nurse, and buy everyday household items. In addition to these traditional role expectations, he has a long list of expectations that are peculiar to his own upbringing.

On Sundays, for example, he may expect his wife to cook a special breakfast while he reads the Sunday paper, and then join him for a leisurely stroll in the park. This is the way his parents spend their

Sundays together, and the day wouldn't feel "right" unless it ech-
oed those dominant chords.

Meanwhile, his wife has an equally long and perhaps conflicting
set of expectations. In addition to wanting her husband to be responsible for all the "manly" chores, such as taking care of the car,
paying the bills, figuring the taxes, mowing the lawn, and oversee-
ing minor and major home repairs, she may expect him to help
with the cooking, shopping, and laundry as well. Then, she, too,
has expectations that reflect her particular upbringing. An ideal
Sunday for her may include going to church, going out to a restau-
rant for brunch, and spending the afternoon visiting relatives.
Since neither of them shared expectations before getting married,
these could develop into a significant source of tension.

But far more important than these conscious or semiconscious expectations are the unconscious ones people bring to marriage,
and the primary one is that their partners, the ones they've win-
nowed out of long lists of candidates, are going to love them the
way their parents never did. ... Once a relationship seems secure,
a psychological switch is triggered deep in the old brain that activates all the latent infantile wishes. It is as if the wounded child
within takes over. Says the child, "I've been good enough long
enough to ensure that this person is going to stay around for a
while. Let's see the payoff." So husbands and wives take a big step
back from each other and wait for the dividends of togetherness
to start rolling in.

— quoted directly from Harville Hendrix, *Getting the Love You
Want: A Guide for Couples*

You can see how the Ladder of Power is probably the number one coaching
tool for fixing relationships. If both partners get on board, and if you combine
the use of this tool with the practice of being your word and having integrity
with your word, you can transform your relationship.

REAL-LIFE EXAMPLE

Setting A National Service Record

MAKING A telephone call to a government department in South Africa and actually having someone answer, then getting a satisfactory resolution to your problem, is a rare occasion. So rare, that people will share it for years to come it the way old schoolmates reminisce rambunctiously about their peak teenage experiences. My story involves the phone company Telkom and illustrates an effective use of the Ladder of Power.

I was living in Newlands, Cape Town, and my landline had been breaking intermittently for weeks. This was the early days of cellular phones and we still used dial-up lines for Internet connectivity, so this was a real problem for my business, which I ran from home.

Each time I'd called, they'd done a remote test and said that the fault wasn't inside the house, but outside on one of the streetside boxes, and that it would be picked up by normal procedural checks and repaired as a matter of course. This should only take a week at most, I was told. Unlike in other provinces, things generally worked in the Western Cape and so I trusted that the information given was correct and my problem would be sorted within the week. It wasn't, and a month later, after four more calls, it still wasn't.

I had seen the Telkom vans tending to the boxes in my area and so clearly the fault wasn't picked up and probably wasn't even there, but inside the house, despite what they were telling me. I decided it would be best for a technician to test the line from inside the house.

I set myself to be prepared to receive "No" for an answer, and called the helpline. "I'm sorry you're the one who's got me on the line today," I said, "but I'm not going to end this call until I have a technician in my house to inspect my line."

"Well we can't make that happen, sir," she replied.

"I understand," I said, with my tone still light and accepting and having my energy set so that she could pick up that I was willing to accept a "No" answer, but that I would still persist on asking a few more times.

I did just that. "I accept that you don't normally doing that, and I'm asking if you will, because it's been six weeks and I just can't go on like this. It's your guy's mistake…"

We went a few more rounds like this. I managed to not lose my cool or get pushy but to just keep asking without giving in, but still letting her know, by virtue of my energy and my tone, that if the answer really did turn out to be "No" I would eventually accept that. Meanwhile, I was going to keep on trying.

Eventually she said what I'd been hoping to hear. "Hold on, let me talk to my manager and see what I can do." I held for about five minutes, listening to a pan flute version of *This Land Is Your Land*. She came back on and said, "We've managed to locate a technician in your area and made a call to him. He should be arriving in the next few minutes."

"Thanks for your help," I said, "would you mind staying on the line with me until they arrive so we can deal with that in the event that it doesn't happen?"

"OK," she said.

Fortunately, it didn't take that long. Within five minutes my intercom rang and, sure enough, it was the Telkom technician. I looked at the time. It had taken forty minutes. To this day I still believe that's a national record!

Once again, using this tool requires that you have an open mind and clear energy before you make any request. The other person needs to feel a sense of autonomy, that if they say yes, it came from them. If they feel forced into saying yes, they'll either resent it and not follow through, or they may well just react and say no. So it's in your interests to give them the permission to say no, and to make sure they really feel that. Giving them permission in this way doesn't mean you can't ask. It means you are, honestly, asking.

8 | Working with Emotions

D O YOU find that you get carried away by your emotions? Do you end up doing or saying things that you regret? Or do you suppress your emotions in order for that never to happen? Or perhaps you're the person who insists that they never experience emotion—except when you get angry with other people being emotional! Then you might be that person who feels guilty for feeling emotions of any kind—especially anger. And you feel guilty a lot.

Emotions are energising. They lead you into action. Those actions can sometimes end up being things that you later regret! What if you could have a choice over how to express your emotions without suppressing them?

In this chapter you'll discover—or learn more about—the energy of emotions. You'll learn to recognise and work with that energy in a constructive way, instead of denying or suppressing it. You'll know what different emotions are trying to get you to do, and you'll be able to do it in a way that is purposeful and constructive.

Chapter Theme Outcomes

Discover or learn more about your emotions and how to manage and direct them in a way that is purposeful and constructive.

By engaging in this chapter you will:

- ✓ Discover how you can deal with the energy of emotions in a nonreactive way;
- ✓ Recognise what core emotions you're experiencing at any one time—and what message that emotion contains;
- ✓ Learn to transform the energy of any emotion and use it for a positive purpose or to fuel a positive action;
- ✓ Know what to do to have this as a first response, especially when you are experiencing high levels of emotion.

Working with Emotions

IMAGINE IF you had no emotions. Life would be a monotonous hum. Or what if you only had the "good" emotions? That would be like not feeling the pain of a toothache. You wouldn't know you had a problem and you'd end up without teeth much sooner than you'd like. Similarly, without fear, you wouldn't know if your life was in danger. Without anger, you wouldn't know that you need to stand up for yourself.

Emotions are not necessarily bad or dangerous, although they can sometimes feel that way. As the psychologist David Barlow points out, "You need the full range of emotions—'good' and 'bad'—to be able to function in the world." In addition, you've already seen that you need those emotions to make good decisions.

So you could say that your emotions tell you important things about the world. To paraphrase Barlow, they help you to navigate it and motivate you to act in ways that are adaptive—and, in some cases, necessary—for your wellbeing, even your survival. Even the person who's apparently always positive and "out there" might benefit from recognising their frustration or anger and allowing it into their life. With this awareness, they'd hopefully be able to channel it in a constructive, purposeful way, for example by making some requests or setting some boundaries in a way that averts burnout.

Similarly, when you're experiencing anxiety, you can check to see if the future threat you're concerned about is real or not. If it's real, then you should get to work making a plan or preparing to deal with it. Perhaps it's a speech you have to write. Or a deadline or sales target you have to meet. And you can also decide what you can and can't change about the situation.

The problem arises when you're not able to separate out what the emotion is trying to tell you—its message—from the experience of the emotion. Without this awareness, you have no choice but to "become" the emotion. That's when your emotions, and not you, start running your life. Getting ahead of your emotions doesn't mean you won't feel anything ever again. It means you'll have some choice and freedom around what you feel and for how long, and how you act in response to those feelings.

A starting point would be to see that emotions are just energy in motion. Without a label or judgement attached, they are neutral, neither good nor bad. There is no need for them to lead to a reaction. Think about it like this: if somebody shouts a warning at you that a car is about to run you over, do you go tell them they've been rude, or do you thank them? There's your clue about how you could treat emotions. You could learn to listen to, or read, the emotion, take its message, say thanks, and move on!

When you do this, you're not suppressing the emotion in a way that means not taking action. You are mindfully, consciously redirecting the energy to fuel a different action. After all, emotions are energy in motion. They energise your thoughts and convert those thoughts into motion. They cause you to act. So, when you read the message in the emotion, you'll find that it can always be expressed as a call to action.

Please note, if the recurrence of an emotion interferes with your ability to function effectively in your daily life, it could be classified as an emotional disorder. If you're experiencing extreme anxiety, phobias, panic attacks, sleep dysfunction or OCD then you should seek help, probably with a cognitive behaviour therapy (CBT) specialist.

The message in the emotion can always be
expressed as a call to action.

If, on the other hand, you don't have an emotional disorder that interferes with your daily life, but you do often act in ways that are not in the best interests of yourself or others—and those behaviours are driven by strong emotions, or by the absence of emotions, then it may be time to look deeper. The table on the next page and the exercise that follows will introduce you to a new way of looking at emotions. This approach has been sourced from the *Unified Protocol for Transdiagnostic Treatment of Emotional Disorders* by David Barlow and adapted by myself and my partner and colleague, clinical psychologist and CBT specialist Dr Colinda Linde.

Interested? Let's move on and find out what the messages are in some key emotions and what you can do about them. Please note that for a more in-depth look at emotions along this axis, you can explore the *Practical Mindfulness* book and online program, listed in the *Further Resources* section at the back.

Key Emotions and Their Messages

Here are six key emotions and their related messages and calls to action, which you can use as a checklist:

Emotion	Message	Call to Action
Anger	A boundary has been violated.	*What boundaries do I need to set?* *How can I act assertively and not aggressively?* *How can I channel this anger into a constructive action?*
Anxiety	There's a future threat, real or imagined.	*Is this threat real? If so, do I fight or flight?* *Is this threat imagined (perceived)? If so, how can I ground myself in reality? What plan do I need to make?*
Frustration	Things are not going my way.	*What do I need in this situation and who do I need to ask?* *What reality am I not accepting about the situation?*
Sadness	I've been hurt / wounded / disappointed.	*Do I need support?* *Do I need to withdraw for a while and regroup?*
Guilt	Have I wronged someone?	*Is there any part of what happened that I need to correct or atone for?*
Joy	Things are going my way.	*Who can I share this with?* *What good can I do with this energy?*

Clearly, when you're experiencing an emotion, getting present and figuring out the message is the last thing you feel like doing—it doesn't even enter your mind. So coming up next is an exercise so you can do some off-the-field practice while you're still calm and sane. Hopefully you'll remember it next time you're on the field of life and experiencing one of those emotions!

PRACTICAL EXERCISE — DO THIS NOW

Find the Message In the Emotion

MAKE A list of some emotions you are currently experiencing (or the last few times you experienced a strong emotion). Use the list in the table on the previous page if you need some ideas or direction.

Step 1 Name the emotion.

1)

2)

Step 2 Ask yourself what the message is inside each emotion.

1)

2)

Step 3 Once you've identified the message, see if you can find the related call to action, expressed as a question. Don't complicate things. Use the table on the previous page as a guide.

1)

2)

Step 4 Define what action you'll take and by when. (Or, what action you could have taken, and will take if it happens again.)

1)

2)

.

THE SCIENCE / THE SOURCE

When Psychology Met Mindfulness —and Coaching

THE FIELD of psychology has developed along two broad, but distinct, paths: one that speculated on the inner workings—or ramblings—of the mind, and one that looked primarily at external behaviours that could be measured. We can put Freud and Jung, both of whom talked about dreams and the subconscious, in the former category and Pavlov, who famously trained dogs to salivate at the sound of a bell, Watson and Skinner, who experimented with rats, in the latter.

While both approaches are valid, the one that focused on external behaviours—known, unsurprisingly, as behaviourism—lent itself more easily to scientific study. Changes in behaviour as a result of a particular intervention, for example, giving a food pellet to a rat, or a sweet to a child, can be objectively measured and, importantly, peer-reviewed.

It's much more difficult—if not impossible—to scientifically verify the progress of a person as they go through psychoanalysis. The outcomes are too nebulous and, in any case, any study would rely on the person reporting on their own progress. That's like relying on an unsupervised worker to be honest about how they've spent their day: highly unreliable from a scientific point of view.

The problem with behaviourism, however, is that human beings do have a linguistic framework—and therefore a more complex inner life—than animals. The thoughts and feelings that make up this inner life do influence outcomes and so a way was needed to access that black box—a way that could be measured.

The field of cognitive therapy emerged as an answer to this problem. It was developed primarily by American psychiatrist Aaron Beck, who noticed what he termed "automatic thoughts" in his clients' and in his own mind. These are the thoughts that arise constantly in your mind—the same thoughts you learn to observe in a mindfulness meditation—and which you can recognise and act upon.

For example, if somebody tells you that your anxiety—and consequent inability to go out at night—is being caused by your fear of sunsets, you can look and see that, in fact, it's being caused by your fear of meeting new people. With the right guidance, you can then make the necessary adjustments and change the behaviour.

Freud, on the other hand, would have insisted that the anxiety was being driven entirely by an "unconscious" urge, like guilt over your secret desire to have sex, and that you as the client simply can't see or have access to those urges. You would have needed to listen to your therapist and accept what you were told about your own "unconscious" urges. Anything you said otherwise would simply have been brushed off as denial or resistance.

Beck's approach—and he was supported by others, like Albert Ellis, Arnold Lazarus and David Barlow—gave people some credit for being able to look into and know their own minds, at least to a degree, and to be able to work effectively with what they found there. You can liken this to being able to see to the horizon from wherever you are on earth right now—you can't see the whole earth, but you can see a fair bit, enough to function and make good decisions, which is all you need.

This evolution of the psychological model meant that, instead of just applying external stimuli to see what happens to the external behaviour, scientists could now work more objectively at a subtler level, at the level of ideas (beliefs, thoughts, cognitions) within the mind. They could apply an idea to a belief and see what behavioural outcome happened as a result. And they could standardise the treatment and measure it across multiple clients in a way that stood up to scientific standards.

Cognitive behaviour therapy (CBT) is the branch of psychology that has evolved out of the work of Beck, and those who followed him. It's referred to as an "evidence-based" approach and can be applied with great effectiveness to managing extreme clinical states of emotion which have become disorders—such as Generalised Anxiety Disorder, Major Depression and others.

In practice, this means that CBT can be used to diagnose and treat an emotional disorder like anxiety, social phobia, OCD, addiction and even depression, within a finite number of sessions. It makes a noticeable difference to actual, observable behaviours, and it can get a person back on their feet without having to go through an interminable process of endless self-reflection.

To this extent there are many similarities between CBT and coaching. The main difference is that coaching doesn't deal with those disorders, but rather with people's functioning and performance outside of any such disorders, and the technical approach of coaching is different. Very often, a person who has become dysfunctional as a result of an emotional disorder might benefit from a combination of CBT and coaching, either simultaneously or sequentially.

Until recently, the emphasis in CBT treatments was on cognitions (your thoughts and beliefs) and behaviours (habits, habitual responses). It was not until the last few years that the role and function of emotion in the development and maintenance of these disorders became emphasised.

This followed the introduction of the Unified Protocol (UP) by David Barlow, who is widely recognised as one of CBT's modern flag-bearers and thought leaders. The UP introduces the concept of emotion-driven behaviours (EDB's) as key to understanding and managing all of the mood, anxiety and addiction disorders. Insight into the nature and function of emotion, the value in grounding yourself during periods of intense emotion, as well as how to regulate your emotions across a range of contexts, is now central to CBT treatment programmes.

In particular, Barlow says this about emotions: "Getting rid of ... uncomfortable emotions would not be very helpful or adaptive and in fact would actually work against you. The truth is that all emotions, even the uncomfortable ones, play very important roles in our lives and provide us with a lot of important information.

"The goal … is not to eliminate uncomfortable emotions like fear, anxiety, sadness, or anger, et cetera. Instead, [you need to] learn how to better understand and tolerate … and manage uncomfortable or distressing emotional experiences and begin to … lead the life you want." This sounds a lot like the objective of coaching—for people with a normal range of emotions that are not disorders, i.e. that do not prevent them from participating normally in life.

In addition, Barlow says, "The only way [you] can determine whether ongoing emotional responses are an accurate reflection of current situational demands or needs, is to anchor [your] awareness within the present context."

Which brings us to mindfulness and why these same behaviourists have come to recognise the importance of mindfulness in supporting people to accelerate their treatment even further. Awareness of thoughts, or cognitions, is naturally key to being able to work with them. Being present in the moment and nonjudgemental enables you to focus your attention on what's real, instead of what's not, and thereby gather better evidence about your reality. Naturally that can make a big difference to conditions like depression, anxiety, phobias, OCD. For example, mindful awareness helps to reduce the ruminating that comes with depression and being nonjudgemental, or objective, helps to reduce the catastrophising that accompanies anxiety. These mindfulness key elements all contribute to—and accelerate—the CBT and coaching process.

Taking a more objective and practical approach to emotions like the CBT-based approach introduced earlier might go against the grain for some people. This would be true, in particular, for those who feel that emotions should be put on a pedestal and felt all the way through to "closure". That state presumably arises when you've exhausted the energy of the emotion by expressing it enough times—and exhausted everybody around you, too!

The coaching approach says that you're only able to sustain the energy of the emotion for those extended periods to the extent that you won't let go of your story about whatever the situation is, or whatever happened. The CBT approach introduced earlier aligns with the coaching approach in that both recognise story as story, both turn your attention to the facts of the situation and both get you to transform the energy of the emotion by taking action towards a constructive outcome or purpose—and thereby move on more quickly without suppressing the emotion.

REAL-LIFE EXAMPLE

Turning Anger into Passion

ANGER IS an emotion that has generally received a bad rap. We teach children from an early age to not be angry, and rightfully so. However, we also throw the baby out with the bathwater, in that we end up not learning how to manage and direct our anger, which is very closely aligned to our life force energy.

If you think of fire, or nuclear energy, it can be used destructively, or constructively. The energy that underlies anger is also neutral, until it gets applied to a constructive or destructive purpose.

The energy that gets released with anger is very powerful. Consider how charged you feel when you're angry. If you can take that same energy and put it to good use, like motivating yourself to go to gym, or finish writing that report, or that book, wouldn't that be useful?

During my coach training, we learned to consciously generate and moderate our anger. At first, the exercise we used was a fictional setting and the anger we generated was the typical reactive anger that we all know.

As we progressed through the program, we learned to generate that same anger consciously, by means of a simple decision, and to use it, for example, to power up your enthusiasm for making a presentation. Like an actor, we learned to turn it on and turn it off, at will. We called this process "turning anger into passion".

This experience showed me that the energy underlying emotions is: (a) real; (b) powerful; (c) neutral; (d) abundant; and (e) available to be used for conscious purposes, if applied mindfully.

Of course, I made all sorts of mistakes when I started out on the journey. I sometimes raised my anger at inappropriate times and scared people. I quickly learned not to do that.

I also noticed that I was very good at turning anger on myself in the form of self-criticism. When I realised this and started to use anger to defend myself instead of attack myself, it initially felt quite wrong, even dangerous. I realised that I had developed some bad habits with regards to my emotions.

As I progressed, I learned to recognise that anger was a useful indicator that a boundary had been crossed and that I needed to defend myself, rather than just agreeing to stupid stuff or turning it on myself. I also learned that it provided fuel for me to honour my commitments, for example, when I said I was going to gym, or that I'd get back to somebody, I could call on that same neutral energy that underlies anger, and get it done.

This became a self-generating cycle and raised my overall level of energy and performance. At times I surprised myself by what I was capable of doing, just by mindfully using this energy.

So now you most likely have a new framework for dealing with emotion. Or you could say that you have the possibility of a new relationship with emotion, one that is constructive instead of destructive. Another way we could phrase this is that you can respond to emotions instead of react. This is more than just semantics. When you react, you have no choice, you just find yourself doing that thing, like pressing send on that angry email. When you respond, you exercise choice in the moment before you act. It's in that moment of choice that you can choose to use the energy of the emotion constructively instead of destructively.

Of course, knowing is one thing and doing is another. When you're experiencing an emotion, you're the last to know and the last thing you feel like doing is exercising choice. You'd be well advised to revisit the exercise in this chapter a few more times to embed this learning. By doing that you'll be giving yourself your best possible chance of doing it when the actual situation arises.

9 | The Red Zone

I F YOU put people together for long enough, sooner or later, someone will start treating something like it's the end of the world. Perhaps they get asked to do something that they think will put their reputation at stake. Or the situation requires that they do something that cuts against the grain for them, either because it *breaks* the rules, or perhaps because it *is* a rule and they *hate* rules. Either way, they seem ready to fight to the death to avoid it.

In fact, we literally say that to them: "It's not the end of the world," or, "You won't die," or, when it's over, we might say, "At least nobody died." Yet for that person going through that thing, it feels like it's the end of the world, it feels like life-or-death.

We each have one or two triggers that put us into that life-or-death space where the fight-or-flight response kicks in. We're going to call that the red zone and you're going to learn about your red zone triggers and behaviours, the role they play in your life and work, and what you can do about them.

Chapter Theme Outcomes

Discover or learn more about that highly reactive emotional state when you go into fight-or-flight mode—the "red zone"—and your "red zone" triggers.

By engaging in this chapter you will:

- ✔ Discover what causes any person to go into the "red zone" where they become rigid and immovable—and perhaps quite emotional;
- ✔ Recognise your own personal indicators for when you're in the "red zone" as well as the triggers that get you there;
- ✔ Learn to presence and ground yourself so that you can return to reality and continue to function in a healthy way;
- ✔ Know how to deal with others when they are in the "red zone".

KEY CONCEPT - TAKE NOTE

The Red Zone

LET'S SAY that not breaking the rules was particularly important in your family system when you were a child. You'd have learned very quickly to not cross that line—to not break the rules. Importantly, you'd have learned it as if it were a life-or-death matter, because that's how it would have seemed at that age. For starters, your father was pretty strong, and, secondly, if they kicked you out of the family, well, you couldn't look after yourself.

Now let's say that for someone else, representing the family in the right way, looking the part, performing well, always coming first, was the most important thing in their family system. They'd have learned very quickly to behave in that way. Once again, they'd have learned it believing that their life depended on always winning, succeeding and looking the part.

When you went to school, and you followed the rules, well, that got you recognition and reward. Perhaps you became a prefect. When that other kid went to school and won every prize they could get their hands on, well, that also got them recognition and reward. Perhaps they became the debating champion, the sports captain, or the dux.

Now let's say you both became lawyers. You're the one who's a stickler for being ethical—in other words, for following the rules. You'd even be willing to forego winning a trial in order to abide by the letter and the spirit of the law. However, the other person might eschew such details. For them, it's about winning at all costs. You can see the types of arguments that you and the other person might have, even—or especially—if you were in the same team, representing the same client.

Let's say the other person suggests that you leave out some critical information—which would mean bending the rules—because that will ensure that you win the trial. If you were that first person, you might freak out at the suggestion. "No," you would say, "we must follow the rules! We must do what's right!" You'd fight as though your life depended on it. Meanwhile, for the other person, the same thing is happening, in the other direction. He or she is also re-experiencing their childhood, where winning—they believed—was what kept them alive because it kept them functioning within the family system.

It's important to recognise that these reactions are not just happening conceptually, but physically in your brain. According to neuroscience, your fight-or-flight response, in the form of an amygdala hijack, kicks in. Your executive function, which enables you to govern your behaviour and treat the situation rationally, shuts down. In fact, when discussing this, I've literally heard at least one client say: "Yes, when that happens, I'm afraid that if I give in, I'll lose my job, my children will suffer, and I'll die."

The end result is that neither party wants to give up their position, because that bears the threat of death for them. Instead, they become locked in a fight to be right, to win, to get their way. Neither one realises that the only reason why they have that fear—and that particular focus of attention—in the first place is because that's what they developed a radar for when they were five years old.

David Barlow, the CBT specialist who was quoted in Chapter 8, has pointed out that you can have a maladaptive emotional reaction based on things that are not real. For example, you can be afraid that you're going to have another panic attack in the mall, just because the first one you had was also in a mall, even though the mall had nothing to do with it. Similarly, although

> *When you recognise this, you become able to treat the situation as it is, and not as you are.*

breaking the rules, or not winning, seemed life-threatening when each of you was a child, it's not any longer. You won't, literally, die. In fact, if you can calm down and look at the situation rationally, you'll probably see that neither one of you is likely to lose your career over the issue either. (Yes, there are exceptions, but they're few and far between. Most times, it's not that big a deal. Most times, it's your ego that's fighting.)

When you recognise this, you're able to presence yourself and think rationally. You become able to treat the situation as it is, and not as you are. Perhaps in one instance, you could accept cutting corners and bending a few rules for the sake of winning the case. I'm not advocating that you go as far as doing something illegal, just that you learn to be flexible where reality allows. After all, whether you like it or not, there are often situations where the greater good is served by a leader making a calculated call that pushes their own ethical boundaries.

Perhaps, in another instance, there is no greater good to be served and the other person could recognise that. They could see that winning would only be for their own sake, and so, if they were to respond instead of react, they could accept not winning this time around.

The point is that each situation is unique and deserves to be treated on its own merits. Being aware of your red zone triggers and behaviours will empower you to do that, instead of always having to get your way (the more extroverted reaction), or always feeling like you'd rather die, or be dead, than have to deal with this or that situation (the more introverted reaction).

Now let's look at what you can do about it.

PRACTICAL EXERCISE — DO THIS NOW

My Red Zone Triggers

YOUR RED zone gets triggered when you feel forced to do something you don't want to do, either because it's against what you see as your core personality, or because it's against your priority of values. Below are two fairly comprehensive lists, one for each category just mentioned.

Core Personality

Your red zone might get triggered when you're expected to participate in a project or activity that rubs up against your core personality because:

Key Factor: Control

a)	It's not under your control;
b)	It's too boring or there are too many rules;
c)	It's likely to fail or damage your reputation.

Key Factor: Rules & Standards

d)	It's unethical, noncompliant, or of a poor standard;
e)	It's unkind or inconsiderate of others;
f)	It's too risky and/or there's not enough information.

Key Factor: Other People

g)	It's noisy, silly, mundane, meaningless;
h)	It's outside your area of specialisation or you haven't had time to prepare;
i)	It's too noisy, busy, aggressive, or conflictual.

Priority of Values

Your red zone might get triggered when someone expects you to participate in or support an activity that rubs up against your priority of values because:

1. It's a family, social or leisure event and you feel it's time to work or study;
2. It's a work obligation when you believe it's time for family, social, sport or leisure;
3. It involves spending money on something that you think is not important or valuable;
4. It goes against your strong spiritual or ethical beliefs;
5. It's plain dumb, stupid, and doesn't involve learning or, alternatively, doesn't have any meaning.

Refer to the two lists above and complete the steps below in order to identify your personal red zone trigger. You may identify more than one.

Step 1 Think of the last time you overreacted by getting angry (asserting yourself) or avoiding something (withdrawing or running away). This is especially easy if someone told you, while you were having that reaction, that it's not the end of the world.

Step 2 Refer to the two lists above and identify what really pushed your buttons in that situation. If you're struggling, spend some time with it, perhaps ask a few people who know you well—especially someone who has witnessed you in those situations.

Step 3 When you've identified your red zone trigger, write it down in the space below. If you can't get it exactly then write down what you think it is and look out for it the next time.

My Red Zone trigger is:

If you're finding it difficult to identify your red zone trigger, know that you're not alone. It can be difficult, especially if it's not an obvious one like breaking the rules, or not winning, or not being in control. It may be the case that you don't have massive emotional outbursts, that you're the quiet, even-tempered type. It may be that you're the "kind", "generous" or "fun" person who's always happy and never wants to do harm, so how could you possibly have negative emotions, or a red zone? In these cases, it may feel uncomfortable to even consider that there could be this dark side to yourself. Likewise, if you're quite introverted, you're more likely to say that everyone else has a red zone, but not you.

If any of these describe you, then take a step back and look again at the things you really don't like doing, or that you're really bad at, and which frustrate you. Look for the things you wish weren't there in the world, whether in yourself or in others. Then think about what happens when you're forced to do, or to deal with, those things. If you're more introverted, or you just don't like to consider the negatives, you might look at situations where you find yourself saying, "I'd rather die [*than do X, or Y, or Z*]." That thing. That's your red zone trigger.

Once you have them, then go back and try the exercise again.

THE SCIENCE / THE SOURCE

The Amygdala and Meditation

THE AMYGDALA acts as the brain's radar for threat. It constantly scans the input it's receiving from the senses for signs of danger. If it perceives a threat, the amygdala circuitry triggers the flight-or-flight response. In modern life there are relatively few physical threats, but plenty of verbal ones. At work and on social media, we see and hear things constantly that threaten our idea of ourselves or how the world should be.

"The amygdala connects strongly to brain circuitry for both focusing our attention [in the case of real physical danger] and for intense emotional reactions," say Goleman & Davidson in *The Science of Meditation*. "The amygdala rivets our attention on what it finds troubling so when something worries or upset us, our mind wanders over and over to that thing, even to the point of fixation." No wonder we become so defensive and immovable when we believe we've been offended!

Conversely, the prefrontal cortex, the most recently evolved section of the brain, manages the reactivity of the amygdala. It's the "guard at the gate". It does a check, evaluates, and decides whether to let the reaction through or not. That guard can have a difficult time when there are angry or anxious hordes at the gate. "When anger or anxiety is triggered the amygdala hijack paralyses executive function," say Goleman & Davidson. In other words, you find yourself reacting without thinking.

Neuroscientists know that the stronger the link (i.e. the greater the number of physical connections) between these two parts of the brain, "the less a person will be hijacked by emotional downs and ups of all sorts". Studies performed and/or evaluated by Goleman & Davidson, and reported in their book, have shown that seasoned meditators' brains "had stronger operative connectivity between the prefrontal cortex, which manages reactivity, and the amygdala". Other combinations of studies showed that [mindfulness] training "did reduce the reactivity of the amygdala", although this was likely to be more of a state effect in the beginning, without long-term practice of meditation.

Long-term meditators showed "both this reduced reactivity in the amygdala plus strengthening of the connection between the prefrontal cortex and amygdala".

These results imply that "when the going gets tough—for example, in response to a major life challenge such as losing a job—the ability to manage distress (which depends upon the connectivity between the prefrontal cortex and amygdala) will be greater in long-term meditators compared to those who have only done [a mindfulness] training.

"The good news is that this resilience can be learned. What we don't know is how long this effect might last. We suspect that it would be short-lived unless participants continued to practice, a key to transforming a state into a trait."

Now that you know what your red zone trigger is, let's move on to what behaviours show up when you're in the red zone. We'll call these your red zone *indicators*, because they'll act as indicators that will support you to become aware of when you're in the red zone.

PRACTICAL EXERCISE — DO THIS NOW

My Red Zone Indicators

YOUR RED zone indicators will usually be in three broad categories: being assertive / aggressive; being compliant; and being withdrawn. These are based on the work of psychologist Karen Horney and area recognised in enneagram parlance as the "Hornevian triads".

Assertive or aggressive reactions may involve micromanaging—it's your way, or the highway. They may also involve trying to get people to do things in a more interesting or exciting way, as their way is seen as being too boring or negative, or in a way that will ensure success, because you suspect that their way is likely to fail and that could damage your reputation.

Compliant responses are likely to involve attempts to align with what's "right". This would probably involve the word *should*, whether you speak it or just think it. For example, you'll hear yourself thinking—or saying—that people *should* align to some or other rules or standards. Those may be ethical standards, quality standards, compliance standards, standards of care and kindness towards others, or standards of caution.

Withdrawn responses will probably involve less overt action and more retreating into thinking and feeling. You're likely to tell yourself that you'd rather die, or be dead, than do that—it's "beneath" you, it's "superficial", it involves all those "idiots" out there, or all that "noise" and "trivia".

If you're doing any of these things in an extreme way—like it's the end of the world if you don't get your way, or like you'd rather die than do that thing— that's your red zone indicator. The more precisely you can identify your behaviour, and especially the particular words or phrases that you think and say during those moments, the better. It will act as an alarm clock so that you can become aware without having to wait for someone else to point it out to you, by which time the damage is already done.

My Red Zone indicator is:

You can support yourself by telling someone about your red zone trigger and sharing your red zone indicator—those behaviours that indicate when you're in the red zone. This should ideally be the people closest to you at home and at work. Then, give them permission to point it out to you when you're doing that thing—when you're in the red zone. Finally, and most importantly, agree to listen to them!

REAL-LIFE EXAMPLE

Annoying Me on Purpose!

THE WAY I grew up, I learned to follow the rules. My father was as tough as they come and he was very active around the home, always fixing and doing things. One problem: I was his helper, and he was a perfectionist, with a temper, so you didn't want to stuff up. You didn't want to make a mistake. You didn't want to not be there when he called or told you to do something. As I said, I learned to follow the rules.

Later on in life, although I rebelled in many ways, I also found it very easy to follow instructions and conform to the rules of a place once I had accepted it. For example, to follow office procedures at work. Naturally I was also good at making the rules. And at making sure people followed the rules.

In fact, when people didn't follow the rules, I could never understand it, and this became a problem. For example, if I was at a place and people were told to fill in forms and go join a queue, but then a bunch of them would not fill out the forms first, but go and mill about where the queue was supposed to be, then decide to push in and the fill out the forms all at the end, just before they reached the table or counter. I'd always be the guy who followed the instructions to the letter and those other people would make me so mad!

Life being a great teacher, I ended up marrying a woman who didn't care much for rules and didn't pay much attention to what I thought were clear agreements, in particular about time. I'd make an agreement with her, say to meet at a particular time, and she'd arrive much later, nonplussed. I'd blow my top. She'd just brush it off as nothing, which would incense me even more. I'd enter the red zone. Sometimes, I'd actually lose my rag and shout. Once or twice I even threw things across the room.

The thing that made me most mad was that I naturally assumed that the other person had the same awareness and set of priorities regarding the rules, or an agreed time, that I had. Therefore, my logical brain concluded, if they didn't conform to those rules, or the agreement, they simply had to be doing it deliberately. And why? Well the only reason could be to annoy and antagonise me. No matter what my ex-wife said to the contrary, I couldn't see it differently. Similarly, at work, when people didn't follow procedures or do things as the system required them to—then I'd get equally annoyed, and once again assume that they must be doing it deliberately to rebel, to send a message, or to annoy me personally.

It was only years later, after studying the enneagram and then debriefing hundreds of people on their enneagram styles, that I learned that there are actually people who simply blank out any awareness of rules or agreements. It's like those instructions or the contracting conversation never happened for them— like that song came on the radio and they never heard it because their attention was elsewhere.

This didn't make it OK for me, but it did enable me to deal with it without getting angry or going into the red zone. I could talk to them about it without making them wrong or assuming they've done it deliberately. Today, those conversations go a whole lot better. Ironically, I'm more likely to get the acknowledgement from them that I'm looking for, because I've learned to talk their language and so they're not actively rebelling against me.

In fact, I'm also better at making the agreements with these rule-breakers in the first place. Most often, I'll do what they do, which is to sell them the idea of what it can do for them in the future if they buy into the agreement. "Your commission will be paid on time if you submit your sales reports right away," works much better than, "You must follow the process and do the paperwork once you've closed the deal, because that's the procedure." Or, if it's about convincing someone to remember and stick to a time agreement, I'll try something like, "The place we're going to will be real fun, so you don't want to be late or you'll miss out!"

What's even better is that while these kinds of people used to be everywhere in my life, I hardly seem to encounter them anymore. Either I'm not getting hooked in and so I don't notice them, or I no longer attract them. Perhaps, having taken the lesson, those teachers have moved on. I guess I should thank them now!

When you recognise that you're in the red zone, your challenge is to let go of the strong preference you have for not giving in. Remember, your preference is so strong that your brain is telling you that you'll die, or that it'll be the end of the world if you're forced to do, or allow, whatever that thing is. This is difficult, if not impossible, to do by addressing the issue through logic or understanding, because that's gone out the window.

The solution is to first apply the mindfulness practice of grounding and presencing yourself, which is explained below. The next step is to recognise that, no matter what happens, you won't die. This sounds simplistic and yet it's important to take it seriously. After all, it addresses the reaction exactly as it's occurring in your brain—as a life-or-death matter.

PRACTICE - SAVE FOR LATER

Exiting the Red Zone

THE STEPS for when you find yourself having a red zone reaction—or amygdala hijack—are as follows:

Step 1 Presence and ground yourself by doing the following:

- a) Place yourself in space and time;
- b) Look outside (actually look—your brain needs this) and see that the sky, the sun and the clouds are still in the sky and will still be there tomorrow;
- c) Look at the room you are in: the floor, ceiling, walls, furniture. Walk over and touch them if you can. Notice how still everything is, and remind yourself that it'll still be there tomorrow;

    d)   Pay attention to your own body—your heartbeat, your breathing—and recognise that you're not doing any of that, it's just happening by itself. Remind yourself that it will still be happening tomorrow.

If these prove insufficient, you can also try this mindful breathing exercise, which is called box breathing:

Breath in for a count of four; hold for a count of four.
Breath out for a count of four; hold for a count of four.
Repeat.

This is designed to break the amygdala hijack. Once you've calmed down, then go back and do the above presencing exercises.

Step 2 Remind yourself that whatever happens in this situation, you won't actually die. It won't be the end of the world. It's just your mind treating it that way, but it's not a real threat. Your identity might suffer, but your body won't. Whatever happens, you'll live to fight another day.

Step 3 Now respond based on what's right and reasonable in the situation, not based on your fears about the situation. Sometimes, you may be right, and you should continue on your course of action; other times, you may need to move in the direction of your fear, relax your stance and take a different approach. For example: you may need to allow people to bend the rules, lower the standards, or miss the deadline; you may need to take a risk, speak up, or wing it. In either case, you won't *actually* die. Unless you will, then don't do it!

When you've managed to successfully exit from the red zone and deal with a situation as it is, instead of as you are, then you'd be well advised to do that thing that human beings are so bad at, which is to gather objective evidence from your actual experience. This is important because the chances are good that you didn't get your way—and so some part of you will be feeling a bit miffed—and yet you survived. If you gather evidence according to that disappointed part of yourself, you'll see the whole exercise as a failure and, the next time, you'll just go into the red zone and do things the way you always did before.

So, instead of asking the question your ego identity wants to ask, which is, "Did it work?" or, more precisely, "Did I get my way?", you can ask yourself, "Did I (we) survive?" The answer is usually yes! Then you might ask, "What did I (we) learn?" You might also ask, "How did things turn out for the better, even if I don't like to admit it?"

By gathering the evidence that you survived, and acknowledging what you learned, you're addressing the problem as it exists, erroneously, in your mind—that it's a life-or-death matter—and you build a case for not falling victim to your red zone trigger in the future.

Having read all this, you may still be wondering, why should I? What difference does it make? Well, think of a tree. It can stand for hundreds of years. Yet a core part of its strength and durability is the fact that it can flex when there are strong winds.

> *When you learn to master the red zone, flexibility replaces rigidity as your survival strategy.*

You'll notice that the suggested course of action for exiting the red zone recommends breaking your core rule, or moving in the direction of your greatest fear. When you do that, you are in fact flexing, like a tree in the wind. You're responding to the situation instead of resisting it. You're flexing instead of snapping. Ironically, flexing is a survival strategy for the tree, and so it is for you. When you learn to master the red zone, flexibility replaces rigidity as your survival strategy.

With greater flexibility, you'll be able to treat each situation based on its own merits. You'll be a more integrated human being and you'll have more freedom of choice in different situations.

Finally, you might find that the practice of grounding yourself and telling yourself that it's not the end of the world seems trivial to you. You might tell yourself that this is silly and can't possibly work, that life is much more complicated than that. After all, your problems are more severe, more complex, and they require a psychologist and years of therapy.

That may be true in some instances. However, more often, it's your ego's identity that doesn't want you to find a simple solution to ending its tyranny. The invitation is to make an honest attempt, and see what happens.

10 | The State of Flow

YOU WERE introduced to the different motivational states in the first chapter and, hopefully, you've been observing your motivational state ever since. In this chapter you're going to put that practical experience to good use when you learn about the characteristics of the state of flow—also known as the state of "optimal experience".

The factors that are present when you're in the state of flow have been scientifically studied. The good news is, they are replicable. That means they can be activated by choice. The bad news is that you can get into the flow state far more often and with many more activities that you would have imagined. Yes, even by washing the dishes! You see, it's not about the activity, but the way that you approach the activity.

In this chapter, you'll learn the principles of action that you can apply to get yourself into the flow state consciously and deliberately. You'll also find out what to do when you're experiencing resistance to getting started with any activity or project and how to recreate the flow state once you're in it. In fact, you'll learn how you can have the state of flow as a way of life.

Chapter Theme Outcomes

Discover or learn more about the state of flow or "optimal experience".

By engaging in this chapter you will:

- ✓ Discover the scientifically proven factors that are present when you're in the state of flow;
- ✓ Recognise when you're not in the state of flow and what obstacles you need to overcome in order to get there;
- ✓ Learn the principles of action that you can apply to get you into the flow state consciously and deliberately;
- ✓ Know what to do to consistently reactivate the state of flow in order to have it as a way of life.

The State of Flow

A LOT has been written about the subject—and the state—of flow, and most people seem to know what it is when you talk about it. Almost everybody, it seems, has had a flow experience at some point in their lives: that "state of joy, creativity and total involvement in which problems seem to disappear and there is an exhilarating feeling of transcendence".

That quote comes from the definitive book on the subject, *Flow: The Psychology of Happiness*, written by Mihály Csikszentmihalyi (pronounced *shik-shunt-mi-hal-yi)*, professor and former chairman of the Dept of Psychology at the University of Chicago. He is generally recognised as the person who lent scientific credibility to—and popularised—the phenomenon, which he also termed "optimal experience".

Perhaps his most remarkable finding is that the state of flow is not random. It arises when a distinctive set of factors are present. Those factors are under your conscious control and so you can deliberately activate the state of flow. The factors that are generally present when one is experiencing the state of flow are:

- **A challenging activity that requires skills** You're unlikely to experience that state of flow while sitting on the couch watching TV. It's more likely to happen while you're engaged in a task that is at the outer range of your level of skills for that task. You need to believe that you have the potential to succeed, and some doubt that you might not (otherwise it's too easy).

- **Clear goals and feedback** The activity is not random. You have clear goals, you know what those goals are, and you get consistent, immediate feedback as to your progress towards those goals. For example, if you're playing sport, you're either hitting the ball and scoring the points or not. If you're playing music, you're either hitting the notes or not.

- **The paradox of control** It's often the riskier activities that elicit the state of flow, eg. mountain climbing, surgery. This is because you are confronted with a doubtful outcome, yet, through your skill level, you're able to influence that outcome. If genuine physical risk is not for you, then any task that is both challenging and important enough can offer this for you.

- **Intrinsic reward (the activity is done for its own sake)** Although the goal may be to win, or to get to the top of the mountain, that goal becomes forgotten for the sake of the experience of doing the activity and doing it well. When this is the case, the activity becomes known as an autotelic activity—one that is done for its own sake. The goal becomes secondary or peripheral to using the activity to learn, improve, stretch your skills, perfect your craft, and so on.

- **The merging of action and awareness** For the reason that it requires all the skills you currently have available for that task, your attention naturally becomes fully absorbed by the current action you are taking. There is no attention left for anything else. This results in two by-products:
    - o **Concentration on the task at hand** In the words of Csikszentmihalyi, "When an activity is thoroughly engrossing, there is not enough attention left over to allow a person to consider either the past or the future, or any other temporarily irrelevant stimuli." This is probably why flow is so enjoyable: your attention is so focused on the task that you forget all your worries.
    - o **The loss of self-consciousness** "One item that disappears from awareness deserves special mention, because in normal life we spend so much time thinking about it: our own self," says Csikszentmihalyi. This temporary suspension of awareness of the self is perhaps another reason why the experience is so enjoyable. It's similar in that sense to what happens when you watch an enthralling movie in a cinema with no distractions. If the task has been sufficiently challenging, then the self is further "enriched by new skills and fresh achievements". This "expansion of the self" clearly adds to the enjoyability of the experience.

- **The transformation of time** Most often, people who have been in the flow state report the compression of time: hours seem to last minutes. Some ballet dancers in Csikszentmihalyi's study reported that "a difficult turn that takes less than a second in real time

> stretches out for what seems like minutes". Either way, the transformation of time into a wholly subjective experience is a by-product of being in flow, while being free from the tyranny of time clearly adds to the enjoyment that you derive from the state.

To summarise, flow arises when there is intense focus at the outer limit of your skill level on a task or activity where the outcome, and the activity itself, really matters to you. This could mean, for example, putting up shelves at home, or creating a mosaic. It could mean hiking, running or cycling a challenging new route. It could imply a career project, like writing a book and getting it published. It requires a goal, and an activity that can provide immediate feedback. It should be an activity that you enjoy or that produces an outcome that you're passionate about.

Author and spiritual teacher Eckhart Tolle uses the word enthusiasm to describe something similar: "Enthusiasm means there is deep enjoyment and what you do plus the added element of a goal or a vision that you work toward." His use of the word enjoyment is specific. By his definition, the joy "does not come from what you do, it flows into what you do". In other words, you will enjoy any mindfully chosen activity, done with full presence, that is not just a means to an end.

"Some things we are initially forced to do against our will turn out to be intrinsically rewarding."—Csikszentmihalyi

---

Tolle's definition points to an important caveat noted by Csikszentmihalyi, who said, "Some things we are initially forced to do against our will turn out in the course of time to be intrinsically rewarding. ... Often children—and adults—need external incentives to take the first steps in an activity that requires a difficult restructuring of attention. Most enjoyable activities are not natural; they demand an effort that initially one is reluctant to make. But once the interaction starts to provide feedback to the person's skills, it usually begins to be intrinsically rewarding." This is well illustrated by one of the world's leading ultra-marathon runners, the South African Bruce Fordyce: he has said that he would run past the second lamppost before he made the decision whether to train each day or not. On a more general level, when you take up running, there is difficulty, pain and stiffness to contend with. Once you start getting fit, you can become enthused by the thrill of challenging your best time.

As you can see, a challenging goal is an essential element for initiating flow. Enjoyment is an input and enthusiasm is an outcome. Activity is the axis. So often, people look for the activity or career path that will "make" them happy. What this shows us is that you can find enjoyment and flow by doing any activity. As Tolle says, "It isn't the action you perform that you really enjoy, but the deep sense of aliveness that flows into it."

Of course, there may be some things you detest, so you're allowed to exclude things. The point is to not sit back and wait until you've figured out which activity you enjoy most. Chances are, you can get into a state of flow while doing any activity.

What's clear is that the flow factors are under your control. You can choose to create activities—and even work scenarios—for yourself that match the first four criteria above, and then invest in them fully. Once you're up and running, the other factors—the merging of action and awareness, the transformation of time—will arise of their own accord and can be promoted through mindful awareness.

This becomes easier as a result of mindful living. "When you make the present moment, instead of past and future, the focal point of your life, your ability to enjoy what you do—and with it the quality of your life—increases dramatically," says Tolle. You might decide to start by applying this at a micro-level, for example by engaging in a hobby on weekends. Then you may choose to expand it into all your activities until it becomes a way of life.

THE SCIENCE / THE SOURCE

The Flowiness of Flow

FLOW SOUNDS like a very unscientific topic. Instead, it conjures up images of 1960s hippies in California just "going with the flow", like, being all groovy, man. However, the term was chosen by Mihály Csikszentmihalyi because that was the word that people most commonly used to describe the state when he began to research it, using scientific methods, in Chicago in the 1970s.

Abraham Maslow had already delved into the subject back in the 1940s, when he identified states that he called "peak experiences". The idea had even older roots in psychology and physiology through the William James protégé, Walter Bradford Cannon, who in the 1900s, identified the fight-or-flight response that was seen to result in heightened levels of performance. Of course, most ancient religions and martial arts forms had long laid claim to such states, and offered practices, such as chanting, or the kata, designed to induce them.

Csikszentmihalyi's research began with various experts—chess players, surgeons, dancers—in and around Chicago and expanded globally to include a vast range of professions and activities: Navajo shepherds, Italian farmers, old women from Korea, teenage bikers in Tokyo. Researchers in Canada, Germany, Italy, Japan, and Australia took up its investigation. It became one of the largest psychological surveys ever conducted.

In the beginning the data consisted of interviews and questionnaires. To achieve greater precision, they developed a technique called the Experience Sampling Method, in which people wore an electronic paging device for a week and wrote down how they felt and what they were thinking about whenever the pager signalled, which was about eight times a day, at random intervals.

By the time he published the second edition of his book *Flow: The Psychology of Happiness* in 2002 (the first edition was published in 1992), over a hundred thousand such "cross sections of experience" had been collected from different parts of the world.

These studies suggested that "optimal experiences were described in the same way by men and women, by young people and old, regardless of cultural differences".

However, a major shortcoming of this research, despite its statistical validity, is that it was based on reported experience. At a scientific level, this is always less desirable than empirical evidence derived from physical measures like heart rate or brainwaves, which are less subject to interpretation or influence by the subject.

Advances in brain imaging technology have changed all that and, as a *Time* magazine article by Steven Kotler pointed out in 2014, the results have shown that the term "flow" was well-chosen: it accurately describes what happens in the brain when the state of flow, or optimal experience, is achieved.

For example, a study of jazz musicians done in 2008, and reported in the aforementioned *Time* article, found that the dorsolateral prefrontal cortex deactivated when they played. That's the area of the brain responsible for self-monitoring, i.e. where your inner critic lives. With that switched off, the mind stops second-guessing and allows the free flow of creativity, automatic problem-solving and risk-taking. The more efficient subconscious, intrinsic processing system takes over.

Further studies reported in the same *Time* article, showed that brainwaves slow down too: from the high-paced beta waves of your normal waking state down to the much slower alpha (daydreaming mode) and theta (pre-sleep mode) waves. This may sound dangerous, but the benefit is that, as in dreams, ideas begin to combine in more radical ways—ways that wouldn't happen when the mind is under conscious control.

Finally, the neurochemistry of the brain has also been shown to change: there is an increase in endorphins, norepinephrine (noradrenaline), dopamine, anandamide and serotonin—a cocktail of performance-enhancing, pleasure-inducing neurochemicals.

As the *Time* article concluded, "Csikszentmihalyi was more right than he could have known. Not only does flow feel flowy; neurobiologically, it actually is flowy."

So now we come to the point of why you were asked in Chapter 1 to pay attention to your motivational state indicators. When you become aware of your motivational state, you can take action—or adjust your current actions—in a way that meets all the elements of flow, thereby potentially igniting the state of flow, or optimal experience. As Tolle says, "You don't have to wait for something 'meaningful' to come into your life so that you can finally enjoy what you do." Essentially, you want to set yourself a task that has a meaningful outcome, which challenges your current skill and risk levels, create some structural tension, like a time limit or a performance parameter—for example, playing a song without missing a single note—and then immerse yourself in it.

When some, more introverted, people experience low motivation as a result of a lack of meaning in their lives, their response is often to withdraw further into themselves, to reflect, or "process", as though the solution might be found by thinking about it. They generally end up in that flat, ennui state. If you remain there, you'll very soon end up feeling depressed.

If that's you, then you're invited to test the veracity of the following statement: "If you haven't solved the problems of the world (or your own problems) within 20 minutes, go and wash the dishes." It sounds trite, but there is a world of truth behind that statement—and, most people report back, it works. Of course, washing the dishes is an analogy for engaging in any activity, but it implies that you start small, with manageable tasks. Ironically, people struggling with low motivation or depression often do have unwashed dishes, and cleaning up your physical environment is a good place to start.

When you do that, you're consciously activating your life force energy by getting into the animated state. This lifts your energy and, once you complete a few tasks, it creates a positive feedback loop. More energy begets more energy. Depression fades away like the mist before the sun.

REAL-LIFE EXAMPLE

Making Monday Great Again

THERE WAS a meme that did the rounds a few years ago that showed a dishevelled, toothless old man, and the caption read: "If Monday was a person." I concurred. I felt like that on a Monday. My Mondays were terrible. I could not take appointments before midday on a Monday and, in fact, preferred to start my sessions on a Tuesday.

Then a client decided that he wanted to kick off the week with some coaching and so asked for a session first thing every Monday morning. I gasped. "OK, I can agree to that," I found myself saying. "It'll have to be via Skype, though," I quickly added. He agreed. I was like that duck, cruising on the surface but paddling like crazy underneath, trying to figure out how I'd be up for an eight o'clock session on a Monday.

I began to reverse engineer what was going on for me. I wasn't doing anything too strenuous on the weekends. In fact, I was relaxing, so what could be the problem? I wasn't even drinking, and if I did, it would be just a couple, nothing heavy and never on a Sunday. Still, there was something missing. I decided it might be water. I drank a heap more water on the weekend before the session. That helped a great deal to reduce mental fog, but my mood was still not quite up there where I needed it to be.

I did my first session and managed to get through it. I noticed that by the time it finished I was feeling quite energised, and much better at nine o'clock on a Monday than I usually did. I got straight into some other tasks and by midday noticed that I was way ahead of the curve for a Monday. By evening I felt energised enough to go for a run, which I usually only got to by midweek.

There was something going on here and I decided to investigate. I eventually found my way to Csikszentmihalyi's findings that people experience the flow state twice as often at work than what they do at home on a weekend. I came across this quote: "The best moments in our lives are not the passive, receptive, relaxing times. ... The best moments usually occur when a person's body or mind is stretched to its limits in a voluntary effort to accomplish something difficult and worthwhile. Optimal experience is thus something that we *make* happen."

That was when it clicked for me. In an attempt to preserve or store up energy, I was slowing down on the weekend, and Sunday afternoon was usually the lowest point of that cycle. I'd want to achieve the most supine state possible by three o'clock on a Sunday. No wonder I was not ready on a Monday and it was such a drag. And I didn't want it to be that way. I had chosen my own career. I was doing what I loved. I wanted to do more of it and do it better. I wasn't working for a boss I hated, and I certainly didn't want to spend my day groaning.

I figured that rest was necessary, but it had to come in another way, and its peak—or nadir—had to come earlier in the cycle. I decided that if I was going to drink or let loose or have a late night, it should be a Friday rather than a Saturday as far as possible. Then Saturday was the day for doing chores, shopping and playing. I should aim for an earlier night on a Saturday and for Sunday morning to be my peak rest time. So, if I was going to sleep in, it should be on a Sunday. If I was going to rest and lie still and not move, it should be on a Sunday morning. Then, by lunchtime, I needed to start moving.

I'd start by cleaning the pool, which is always a kind of active meditation. Then I'd do something like a sorting task. Perhaps to tidy a shelf in the garden shed, or move those boxes in the garage—nothing too heavy, and not getting tempted into a bigger task, just enough to get me moving and find myself in that flow state even for a few minutes. Then it would be a quick check of my work emails—again, just enough to get me going, not getting drawn into any major tasks—except sometimes. Finally, I'd go for a run and a short gym session. I'd really push myself when doing that, because I'd know it's not going to extend into a bigger task and it's going to help me to sleep well.

I found that by Sunday evening I was starting to feel quite revved up and ready for the week and on Monday I'd hit the ground running. Yes, indeed, I'd made my Mondays great again!

At the risk of overstating it, flow is an active process. It requires initiation by decision, followed by sustained action within certain parameters, i.e. challenge and concentration. However, as you've seen, you often don't feel like doing the activity that is required to generate the state of flow. If it's not the wrong activity, it's the wrong time. Or the weather, or other conditions, are wrong. For example, you wanted to go running, but now it's raining. You wanted to check those emails, or write that report, but it's a Sunday and you just shouldn't have to; you just don't feel like it. In most instances, the conditions don't matter. You can run in the rain. You never really feel like checking emails on a Sunday.

Remember, your ability to decide and to act is independent of your thoughts and feelings. The bungee jumper standing on the side of the bridge doesn't feel like it and doesn't think it's such a good idea anymore. Yet she can still jump. In fact, you might even say that passing through some kind of a dip, or overcoming some kind of resistance or inertia, is a necessary condition for initiating flow. The fact is, you almost never feel like getting started with any activity. Yet you can do it.

If you gathered better evidence from your experience,
you'd probably learn to appreciate work more.

Once again, how many times has it happened to you that you did something you didn't want to do, or at a time that didn't seem to suit you, and it turned out to be fun, or a total flow experience? This is an important point. We're very poor at gathering evidence from our experience. If we did, we'd notice what Csikszentmihalyi found: that we get into the flow state twice as often at work than we do at home. And yet, what's everybody trying to do? Get to Friday! Then what happens? Monday comes and you have to drag yourself back to work. You think it's because of the week ahead, but it's because you've gone off the boil! Look what happens to you: by Tuesday you're starting to hum and through all of Wednesday and Thursday you feel much better. Come Friday, you feel great. You think it's because you've got the weekend coming up, but guess what? The challenges and opportunities to focus your efforts that work has provided all week have put you in the flow state more often than not!

Now, if you gathered better evidence from your experience, you'd see this and you'd probably learn to appreciate work more. You'd see it for what it is: an opportunity to get into the flow state. Flowing from that you'd see it as an opportunity to grow and develop as a person, an opportunity you wouldn't have if you were unemployed and moping around at home, or on some eternal holiday!

So, if you're seeking motivation, try gathering better evidence and having less of a story about work and tasks versus leisure. Then use that data to change your relationship to life, work and rest.

11 | The Habit of Completion

DO YOU often find that you have so much to deal with and you don't know where to start? Do you sometimes wonder exactly where your stress is coming from, but you can't quite put your finger on it? When a high level of stress goes on for too long, you eventually accept it as normal.

It may seem crazy to think that a large part of your stress is self-induced and that you can do something about it without changing your whole life. Well, what if that were true? Wouldn't you want to find out? Be careful now, because it's not going to involve rest, at least not in the beginning. In fact, you might want to remember that phrase used by the Stoics: "Not life's events, but one's feelings about those events determine one's happiness."

In this chapter you'll discover—or be reminded of—just how much not prioritising and not getting things done compounds your experience of life as being stressful. You'll learn a simple method for recognising when you're letting those stress-inducing incidents pile up, and what you can do, firstly, to reduce them, and then to keep them at a minimum.

Chapter Theme Outcomes

Discover one of the main sources of stress and how to deal with it.

By engaging in this chapter you will:

- ✓ Discover one of the main sources of stress;
- ✓ Recognise when you're letting stress-inducing incidents pile up;
- ✓ Learn a simple practice that will enable you to eliminate this source of stress and keep it at a minimum;
- ✓ Know what causes you to resist that practice, and what you can do to let go of that resistance and develop it into a habit.

The Habit of Completion

YOU KNOW that experience of having too much to do and not knowing where to begin? For some people that happens occasionally, when the demands just get too much, and it's a temporary thing. For many people, this can be an ongoing experience.

The primary cause of that experience, especially when it's more chronic than acute, is that you've just left too many things undone—you have too many incompletions. You've let things pile up until your demands far outweigh your resources. That in itself is demotivating, and that adds momentum to the spiral.

Think about this scenario: you said you'd call someone, and you didn't. Months later, you see them at the mall, and you remember that incompletion. It comes up in your mind. Whereas, if you'd called them, nothing would come up.

These incompletions lead to further incompletions. You need to call someone for a business reason, but you put it off because you know that you first need to resolve an earlier misunderstanding with that person. One thing leads to another and soon you have a heap of incompletions. It even becomes normal to you, so you don't notice them piling up. Then, if you ever do decide to sort them out, you don't know where to begin.

Other examples of incompletions include: clutter (physical, digital, mental); postponements (repairs, phone calls, admin tasks, all the stuff you've been putting off until tomorrow); broken promises (things you said you'd do but haven't done—every single one gets remembered and processed from time to time); relationship stuff (misunderstandings, unresolved arguments).

In addition, you'll notice that those incompletions occupy a large chunk of your attention. They tend to come up quite randomly, too, at times when you least want them to. Incompletions therefore reduce presence. You also know that they'll require energy or resources to deal with them, and so they can be demotivating when there are too many in front of you. All of this becomes a downward spiral.

Conversely, when you deal with all that stuff—when you create completion, in other words—you gain more and more mental clarity. You gain presence, and the energy to do more. You quickly learn to recognise the things that will lead to incompletions and you pounce on them. This becomes an upward spiral—then a habit, a way of life.

So either way, whether you're allowing incompletions, or doing the opposite—creating completion—it gathers momentum and becomes either a downward or an upward spiral. The obvious question arises, which spiral do you want to be in?

There are two phases to being able to live at the frontier of completion: creating completion and maintaining completion. Below are some exercises to support you to achieve both.

PRACTICAL EXERCISE — DO THIS NOW

Creating Completion

MARK Y for all those things that are complete. In other words, they're sorted. Mark N for all those things that are *not* complete, that you *need* to get sorted. Then say what you'll do, and by when you'll have done it.

Area of Life	Subcategory	Complete?	If not complete, do what, by when?
General Are you sorted (complete) in these areas? If not, what do you need to do, and by when will you do it?	Household clutter	Y / N	
	Business clutter	Y / N	
	Digital clutter	Y / N	
	Physical storage	Y / N	
	Digital storage	Y / N	
	Personal admin	Y / N	
	Personal projects	Y / N	

Area of Life	Subcategory	Complete?	If not complete, do what, by when?
Support Do you have outstanding to-do items in these areas? If not, do you have people you can turn to?	Doctor(s) Lawyer Accountant Coach Handyman Mechanic	Y / N Y / N Y / N Y / N Y / N Y / N	
Order Areas Are you sorted (complete) in these areas? If not, do what, by when?	Workspace Books Music Photos Clothing Tech equipment	Y / N Y / N Y / N Y / N Y / N	
Relationships All good? If not, what issues do you need to resolve?	Unkept promises Changed agreements Unresolved arguments Resentments Unforgiven stuff Withholds	Y / N Y / N Y / N Y / N Y / N Y / N	
Balance All good? If not, what do you need to put in place?	Spouse / Kids Family / Friends Health / Fitness Learning / Growth Leisure / Social	Y / N Y / N Y / N Y / N Y / N	

Maintaining Completion:
Taking A Mindful Completion Walk

TAKE A mindful walk for 20-40 mins in a safe, comfortable place. Perhaps your garden, a familiar park, or a courtyard at work. Stay present by paying attention to your physical environment. Notice everything that comes up to distract you or that occupies your attention. Note it down and make a plan to complete it.

As an alternative to taking a walk, you may choose to be mindfully present while you sit in traffic and use voice memos to record the same.

When you're operating at a high level of completion, your mind will tend to sort through the clutter of life quite efficiently. Much more efficiently than it would when you're incomplete and therefore having to write long, comprehensive lists and driving yourself crazy trying to tick off all the items on that list.

This is especially true if you combine the habit of creating and maintaining completion with a good understanding of the distinction between what's important (those actions that take you towards your main goal) and what's urgent (all the stuff that's coming in that everyone else wants you to do yesterday, and which you can probably delegate, or deprioritise, or downright ignore). In addition, you can create another filter by regularly asking yourself an active open question, like, *What's the next most important thing for me to focus on?* Just like the Kilimanjaro example, this will alert your mind as to what to look out for.

THE SCIENCE / THE SOURCE

Stress: Demands and Resources

AS WITH anything in life, stress is not all bad. In fact, as my co-founder in the *Practical Mindfulness* program, Dr Colinda Linde, stated in her doctoral thesis, "Physiologically, the complete absence of stress is equivalent to death." OK, so we're not going there. Instead, as Colinda is always quick to point out, what you're really driving towards is an optimal level of stress.

To quote her thesis—which measured stress and anxiety levels in cancer patients—again, "The aim … is to manage the degree of stress one encounters effectively, thereby functioning at an optimal level of arousal. Such a level would entail the individual being in balance, where stress is a positive resource versus a hindrance and precursor to illness."

According to Colinda's Demands v Resources model, "You find that stress is present when things are out of balance, in favour of an external force that's been exerted. In human terms, this happens when the many demands that are coming at us from so many sources exceed the available resources."

Demands would include, for example, the volume of tasks at work, multiple demands at home, like financial pressure, young children, a problem relationship, and a family member with a chronic illness, plus your own health and need for leisure and/or study time. If these were to occur all at once, that would equate to a high demand level.

These demands can be classified as acute (short-term), chronic (ongoing) and hassles (small individually, but taken together they mount up). The human body is equipped to deal with acute (short-term, in-the-moment) stressful situations: it activates the fight-or-flight response. However, the effects of chronic (long-term, ongoing) stress are more dangerous to physical and mental health than are those of most acute stressors.

Chronic stress results in the release of a different range of stress hormones, which trickle out constantly over many months, and are being associated more and more with severe illnesses such as cancer, fibromyalgia, lupus and arthritis. There is also a relationship between chronic stress and depression.

It's important, therefore, to do something about chronic stress, even though it's the one we're most likely to ignore. The habit of creating completion and the long-term practice of meditation are two valuable, proven solutions.

The coping resources you might be able to draw on to deal with these demands would include things like basic needs such as food and shelter being provided for; a strong support system including some combination of parent, sibling, friend and/or therapist; your own good health; a sense of humour; and so on.

An important distinction to consider when it comes to resources is real versus false resources. For example, when you're feeling tired, a cup of coffee or a piece of chocolate may give you a temporary lift. However, once the effect has worn off, it may leave you feeling even worse. If your response is to then reach for another false resource, you can see what kind of roller-coaster you can get yourself onto.

It may be appropriate to reach for some temporary relief when you're under pressure, however, any temporary solution that is used as a substitute for a real solution could be termed a false, or fake, resource.

Creating completion is clearly a valuable resource in your stress armoury. It's a resource that eats up demands for breakfast—a bit like a white blood cell that eats up bacteria. It's important to reiterate the point that completion can supersede the need for long lists and for hypervigilance. When you're present enough and your mind is clear enough, problems will rise to the surface in time for you to catch them. This applies in your individual as well as in your family and work life.

Often when there are problems, we look around for someone to blame, and then seek to put a process in place to make sure it never happens again. Sure, there are times when that's necessary and relevant, however, consider that things will always happen that no process could have caught. So perhaps the better response is to say, "Oh, good, we caught that." Of course, you did, you were all present and paying attention.

If you practice creating and maintaining completion, and inspire the people around you to do the same, you'll have this as your experience more often than not. Problems will become small bumps in the road, instead of great, big, threatening catastrophes.

REAL-LIFE EXAMPLE

Denuding A Great Library

SOON AFTER I first learned about completion, I found myself sitting in my study and looking at all the books I had accumulated. I had hundreds of them—and just as many in the lounge downstairs. And those were only the ones I'd unpacked since our last move. There were still more in boxes in the garage.

I'd read a great many of them, but probably more than half had been bought in one of those mad bookshop moments I used to have, when I was convinced that I had to read *this* book as well as the original one I'd chosen and so I'd add it to the pile.

Now, whenever I looked at those books, I felt the pressure of having to get through them all. I recognized that each time I sat in my study, even though I might be there to focus on work, this whole gestalt arose out of the presence of those books and created a background noise that raised my stress levels.

Putting them into the garage wasn't going to work. I'd still see the boxes every day. Renting a storeroom would end up being more expensive after a few months than if I bought each book again when I finally had the time to read it. So, I made the decision to clear out all the ones I had not read plus all those I was not going to read again or use for reference, including the ones that were just cool to have on my bookshelf. I took some to second-hand bookshops and the rest to charity.

I kept those that I had read and which I was sure I would use for future reference, plus my top 20 fiction books that I was sure I would read again, or dip into for sheer wonderment and pleasure. I also decided that in future I would only buy one book at a time and only if I was sure I had the time to read it—and that meant measuring not just the desire or intention, but my actual capacity given what else I had going on at the time—and what else I was still reading. Anything else, I had to face it, I simply didn't have time for.

During my monitor-and-record exercises a short while after that, I noticed that I was no longer feeling that background pressure as a result of all the reading I needed to do. Instead, I felt like a weight had been lifted. I noted that this completion stuff really works!

You can see that creating and maintaining completion brings together many elements of this program. It's about knowing yourself and your values, knowing what's important to you. Then it's about being your word, being ready to pounce on things and do them, just because you said so. That requires quick and consistent decision-making and having no story. It means managing and directing your emotions, readily converting the energy of emotions into constructive, purposeful action. It means taking responsibility for what you want and asking for it; then taking what you get and not taking what you don't get. In addition, it means activating the flow principles: bringing your full, non-judgemental attention to every task in a way that activates the flow state.

It's about being your word, being ready to pounce on things and do them, just because you said so.

Of course, it also requires that you gather accurate and objective evidence from your experience. After all, nobody feels like doing those small tasks. There's always something else you can do—something apparently more valuable, more entertaining or enjoyable, less trivial. Yet those tasks remain, and they continue to take up space in your mind. Instead, try completing those tasks, and record, like a scientist with a clipboard, how you feel afterwards. You'll be surprised at what you find. At the very least, by gathering evidence, you'll build a case for doing it again and that will lower your resistance for the next task. It will get easier and easier to do.

When you live like this you enjoy many benefits. You keep the flywheel spinning, and so your energy remains high. Your mental clarity is a cut above the rest. Likewise your level of presence, and you know what they say about presence: the attention goes to the person in the room who is most present. Presence is a major contributor to what people see as charisma.

Now, if that doesn't inspire you to practice creating and maintaining completion, nothing will!

12 | Legacy & Lifestyle

OST PEOPLE don't have a defined legacy, and many have never consciously defined what experience of life—and therefore what lifestyle—they'd like to have. No wonder, then, that they spend their lives complaining!

Consider everything you've learned in this program, from your personality and values, to your power to create, the power of decision and commitment, the importance of taking responsibility for what you want, not being in story, and the principles for getting into the flow state. The next logical step towards personal effectiveness must surely be to consciously define what you want your life to be about, and then to take action towards achieving it.

By participating in this chapter, you'll get a chance to define your legacy and set lifestyle goals. You'll be able to plan what you need to do in order to achieve those goals. You'll also be introduced to a daily practice that will keep you on track to maintain the lifestyle and to achieve your legacy goals.

Chapter Theme Outcomes

Develop your own legacy and lifestyle statement.

By engaging in this chapter you will:

- ✓ Discover the importance of a legacy and lifestyle statement for effective decision-making;
- ✓ Develop your own legacy and lifestyle statement;
- ✓ Define a daily check-in practice that will enable you to consistently reference your legacy and lifestyle statement;
- ✓ Recognise when you're not being or acting in integrity with your leadership brand statement and know what to do to correct that;
- ✓ Assess your level of achievement of your main goals and complete your participation in this program.

My Legacy & Lifestyle Statement

LET'S FACE it, life is not as simple as it used to be, and the old rules don't apply anymore. Think about it: a generation or two back, your place in society was quite well-defined in terms of race, religion, social class and gender. Whether you were the first-born son of an English aristocrat or the third daughter of an Indian municipal clerk, either way, the parameters of your life path—who you could marry, what work you would do—were, to a greater or lesser degree, handed to you. Likewise, your moral behaviour choices, the way you would raise your children, even your choices at the food market and how to spend your leisure time, were fairly limited.

In the post-consumer, post-truth, social media age, we're overwhelmed by choice. Women can become engineers or pilots as much as men can be openly gay and hold political office. Deciding on a career can be a major challenge, compounded by the fact that many people are now likely to have multiple careers across the span of their lifetime. Teenagers today have a range of gender identities available to them that were not even named a generation ago. That's not to mention the range of spiritual, religious, leisure and entertainment choices; the range of news sources; the range of product options; the relative ease with which one can travel and even emigrate.

That means, quite simply, that there are many more decisions to be made and, unlike the days of yore, they are not being handed to you by social or religious norms. Who, or what, do you reference?

To answer that question, let's look again, as we did in Chapter 5, at when you get up on a weekday morning, and you have to get the kids to school and yourself to work. Your priorities and decisions are handed to you by the very clear and tight deadlines you have, and to which you are committed. Conversely, when you wake up on a Sunday morning and there are no plans, and no deadline, you can debate endlessly about what to do. As you saw, this illustrates the point that the more clear your context is, the more the decisions just present themselves, there's no debate needed.

So, let's bring this together with the previous point. We talked about this crazy new world with its dearth of reference points. That means a dearth of context for decision-making. The solution? You have to create your own. And the best way to do this is to create a clear legacy and lifestyle statement. Your legacy statement will include the standards that you choose to live by and therefore the example you choose to set for those who follow after you. It's about defining and then living out those things you'd like people to say about you after you've gone. It can also include a statement of the contribution you choose to make to society, or the world.

A legacy statement will give you a strong reference point for the decisions you need to make in this topsy-turvy world. You can reference it for decisions about who you are and how you choose to respond to situations. For example, are you going to get angry with your child, or demonstrate the behaviour that you want them to emulate? Refer to your character standards in your legacy statement. You can also reference it for how to deal with challenges and opportunities that come your way. Are you going to get involved in some dodgy deal, or does that go against your legacy statement? And so on. Naturally, this goes together with a commitment to live in integrity with your word. Hmm, it's not easy.

> *A legacy statement will give you a reference point for the decisions you need to make in this topsy-turvy world.*

In addition, when you make a commitment to a clearly defined outcome, not only new thoughts, but also new feelings arise. When you committed—hypothetically—to climb Kilimanjaro in six months' time, you felt not only a little scared, but also tremendously inspired, didn't you? That illustrates a point that's best summed up by the following statement: *Who you are is determined by the future you're committed to.* If you're bored, it's most likely because you're committed—or resigned—to a boring future. If you want to be inspired, well then you need to commit to an inspiring future.

I've coached many people, especially men, who've attained their great goal of selling their business for large sums of money and retiring early. They come to me when they've become bored, disillusioned, even depressed. The answer is usually that they need a new and inspiring future that they can commit to. Since it can't be about money anymore, it has to be about something else. Some choose to start a philanthropic foundation, while others become angel investors. Whatever they choose, they have to create it out of nothing and set a goal big enough that it scares them, or that they might never achieve it in this lifetime. Anything less just doesn't work. Then they have to commit to the path. Most often, this shift is enough to get them feeling inspired again.

Wouldn't you want to live every day of your life feeling inspired? An inspiring legacy and lifestyle statement—supported by a strong commitment to live that statement, and to be your word—can give you that. In order for your legacy statement to be inspiring, you'd have to set yourself some standards and goals that you find a little scary, yet also inspiring, to live up to. to see your children and descendants living in. To truly inspire you, it should be almost, or perhaps, not achievable in this lifetime.

THE SCIENCE / THE SOURCE

Consciousness & Intention

"BECAUSE NO branch of science deals with consciousness directly, there is no single accepted description of how it works," says Mihály Csikszentmihalyi, former professor of psychology at the University and Chicago and the person who led the studies into the state of flow.

Csikszentmihalyi advocates a "phenomenological model of consciousness based on information theory". This means a model that deals directly with events—phenomena—as we experience and interpret them, rather than focusing on the anatomical structures, neurochemical processes, and so on, while adopting principles from information theory.

In other words, if you could shine a light on your thinking, you would see that you think using words. It doesn't matter that there are axons and dendrites and so on. What you experience is a never-ending stream of thinking that takes the form of words.

"With this framework in mind," says Csikszentmihalyi, "[being conscious] means that certain specific conscious events (sensations, feelings, thoughts, intentions) are occurring, and that we are able to direct their course." How do we do that? As you've seen, by using words. By placing words into the stream of words that already exists rather randomly and chaotically in your mind.

Csikszentmihalyi continues: "Thus we might think of consciousness as *intentionally* ordered information. … We may call *intentions* the force that keeps information in consciousness ordered." The emphasis using italics is mine. What is an intention? It's what you create when you give your word using a speech act.

"The intentions we either inherit or acquire are organized in hierarchies of goals, which specify the order of precedence among them," he says. This is what we pointed to when we looked at values. "Most people … adopt 'sensible' goals. … But there are enough exceptions in every culture to show that goals are quite flexible. Individuals who depart from the norms—heroes, saints, sages, artists, and poets, as well as madmen and criminals—look for different things in life than most others do. The existence of people like these shows that consciousness can be ordered in terms of different goals and intentions. Each of us has this freedom to control our subjective reality." Once again, how do we do that? By organising our thoughts using words. Are we limited in terms of what words we can use or how we can organise them? No, we are not!

"One of the main forces that affects consciousness adversely is psychic disorder—that is, information that conflicts with existing intentions, or distracts us from carrying them out." In other words, when you don't feel like it anymore, or don't think it's a good idea anymore. "All these varieties of disorder force attention to be diverted to undesirable objects, leaving us no longer free to use it according to our preferences. Psychic energy becomes unwieldy and ineffective." We become distracted. We watch TV instead of writing that report we said we would.

"The opposite state from the condition of psychic entropy is optimal experience. When … awareness is congruent with goals, psychic energy flows effortlessly. … The positive feedback strengthens the self, and more attention is freed to deal with the outer and the inner environment." Here he's pointing to what we've called being in integrity with your word.

"The 'battle'," he says, "is not really *against* the self, but against the entropy that brings disorder to consciousness. It is really a battle *for* the self." By this last statement, Csikszentmihalyi means it is a battle to create your own unique self in the face of all your conditioning and all the social forces that act on you and in reaction to which you feel a pressure to conform. He calls this process—of creating your own unique self—differentiation, which could be likened to Jung's concept of individuation.

How do you do that, consciously? Through the application of the word, just as we've done here.

If you were paying attention, you'll see that by creating a legacy and lifestyle statement, you'll be adding that structural tension that was introduced in Chapter 10 as the key component for generating the state of flow—except, in this case, you'll be adding it not just to small tasks, but to your whole life!

In addition to handing yourself a clear context for decision-making and for generating a sense of inspiration at the broadest level, when you move from the legacy level to the lifestyle level, you'll also hand yourself a myriad more opportunities to generate a flow state. This will happen when you define outcomes for each area of life, those areas you came to recognise in Chapter 3, when you looked at your priority of values. When you make the effort to achieve your desired outcomes in each of those areas, you'll naturally break that down into tasks and those will provide the building blocks for you to consistently generate a state of flow. When you do that, you'll gain all those benefits that you learned about in Chapter 10.

REAL-LIFE EXAMPLE

Writing Lines for Reward, Not Punishment

YOU'VE PROBABLY seen or heard testimonies of people who've created a vision board and it came about with great precision. Perhaps, you tried it yourself and it didn't work out. Then you decided that those success stories were down to random luck, or that they were just poppycock, and you gave up.

Sure, we humans are not perfect manifestors. If you were, you'd have a problem. You'd think "elephant" and there'd be an elephant in your lounge. That wouldn't work. Fortunately, you have to try harder than that. You have to do it many times and with great consistency and focused attention. Then both you and whatever forces deliver on these things can be sure that they've got the order right—that an elephant is really what you're after.

Of the many things I've tried, one of the best is the good old-fashioned writing of lines, just like the teachers made you do in school: *"Write, I will not be late, one hundred times on the board!"* In fact, studies have shown that writing notes by hand increases learning and retention rates. It seems that there's something about the physical act of writing that creates a more stable map in the brain than simply thinking about it or typing it out.

When I started out as a coach, and needed to build a regular income, I spent an entire year writing lines. It was a short statement, consisting of three sentences, that stated, in the present tense, a career goal I was aiming for. For the sake of example, I'll make one up here: *I am a successful entrepreneurial coach. I am invited and paid to speak around the world. I work on average 20 hours a week and earn $10,000 a month.* I bought a Moleskin notebook and wrote down that paragraph three times, every morning before I started my day.

When I finally did my annual income statement for that year, about a month after the year-end, I wasn't looking for the number I had inserted. Rather, I became absorbed in giving the task my full attention and turning it into a flow experience. Of course, what else did you expect? Ha ha.

The significant fact is that when I finished, and divided the total by 12, my average earnings for that year came within a single dollar (it was in South African rands, actually) of the number I'd been writing down!

Now, it's important to note that I didn't put a crazy number down. It was just a reasonable, responsible number, with a moderately ambitious stretch. However, in my business, there is a great deal of risk and uncertainty, so for me to hit my target earnings in that was not an insignificant feat. On reflections, there were many incidents in the year that I could point to where I didn't get a deal, but another one came through. Or a contract went on for longer than expected. And so on. It's impossible to prove, but I say that expressing this intention in this way played a major part in bringing it about.

One more thing: it's not magic. Writing lines is a long, slow process and while you're doing it you have time to think—and feel. If you do it consciously, you can observe what thoughts and feelings come up while you're writing. You might notice a feeling of despondency arising, and you might recognise that you're not really believing that the goal is possible, at least not today. Then you can coach yourself. *What's standing in your way? What needs to happen for you to shift that belief?* And so on.

So, it may have been more about the self-coaching that arose while I was writing those lines, rather than any magical attractor field that exists out there, but either way, it's a good practice if you're serious about achieving a particular result.

PRACTICAL EXERCISE — DO THIS NOW

My Legacy & Lifestyle Statement

THE EXERCISE that follows will provide a template for you to begin to create your legacy and lifestyle statement. There is no absolute on how to do this or what to include and so the elements provided are a guideline. You may choose to do them all and use it as is. You may also choose to leave some out and add some of your own. You'll probably also want to transfer it into a format that works for you—perhaps typed into a digital format that you can refer to on your phone or tablet, or written up by hand into a notebook that you refer to each morning, or even typed and printed and stored in a folder. Either way, you should keep it accessible and refer to it regularly—daily, if possible. This is a living document and you'll want to revise it as you go.

The exercise also includes a *Create My Day* template, which you can use to guide your daily check-in process, part of which will be to refer to your legacy and lifestyle statement. You should treat this template in the same way as described above for the main statement—transferring to the best format that works for you and storing it where you can access it easily.

In conclusion, and before you move to the exercise, consider these inspiring quotes:

"I went to the woods because I wished to live deliberately, to front only the essential facts of life, and see if I could not learn what it had to teach, and not, when I came to die, discover that I had not lived." —*Henry David Thoreau*

"There is a vitality, a life force, an energy, a quickening that is translated through you into action; and because there is only one of you in all time, this expression is unique. If you block it, it will never exist through any other medium and it will be lost. The world will not have it. You must keep that channel open. It is not for you to determine how good it is, nor how valuable. Nor how it compares with other expressions. It is for you to keep it yours, clearly and directly."—*Martha Graham, dancer and choreographer*

"We find greatest joy, not in getting, but expressing what we are. Men do not really live for honours or for pay; their gladness is not in the taking and holding, but in the doing, the striving, the building, the living. It is a higher joy to teach than to be taught. It is good to get justice, but better to do it; fun to have things, but more to make them. The happy man is he who lives the life of love, not for the honours it may bring, but for the life itself."—*RJ Baughan*

"This is the true joy in life, the being used for a purpose recognized by yourself as a mighty one; the being a force of nature instead of a feverish selfish clod of ailments and grievances complaining that the world will not devote itself to making you happy. I am of the opinion that my life belongs to the whole community and as long as I live it is my privilege to do for it whatever I can. I want to be thoroughly used up when I die, for the harder I work, the more I live. I rejoice in life for its own sake. Life is no 'brief candle' to me. It is sort of a splendid torch which I have a hold of for the moment, and I want to make it burn as brightly as possible before handing it over to future generations."—*George Bernard Shaw*

Template: My Legacy & Lifestyle Statement

USE THIS worksheet to create your legacy and lifestyle definitions. For each element, select from the options given, plus add one or more of your own. Then write out your full sentence at the end. For example, for #2 My Pledge / Personal Code, you might end up with something like, "My commitment is to be *an inspiring leader* and *an active citizen* who always seeks to *lift people's belief in their own possibilities* and *improve the working and living conditions for ordinary people*," where you selected the first three options from those given and added the fourth as your own unique creation.

My Character Standards

Some words that describe my character and that I'm prepared to live by:

☐ Wise	☐ Honest	☐ Brave
☐ Fierce	☐ Friendly	☐ Independent
☐	☐	☐
☐	☐	☐

Write out your selection of character standards:

My Pledge / Personal Code

Who I'm committed to be (how I'm committed to consistently show up in the world, no matter what's going on around me):

My commitment is to be...

<table>
<tr><td>☐ an inspiring leader</td><td>☐ an engaged parent</td></tr>
<tr><td>☐ an active citizen</td><td>☐ a friendly neighbour</td></tr>
<tr><td>☐</td><td>☐</td></tr>
<tr><td>☐</td><td>☐</td></tr>
</table>

who always seeks to...

☐ lift people's belief in their own possibilities.

☐ raise people's expectations of themselves.

☐ spread copious amounts of joy.

☐

☐

☐

Write out your Pledge / Personal Code here:

My Personal Vision

My great life/career goal (expressed as a tangible or living thing that I would like to put into the world and which will hopefully outlive me):

I'm committed to

- ☐ achieve
- ☐ create
- ☐ produce
- ☐ make
- ☐
- ☐

...a / an / the...

- ☐ happy
- ☐ successful
- ☐ educated
- ☐ eco-friendly
- ☐ sustainable
- ☐ profitable
- ☐
- ☐
- ☐

...

- ☐ family
- ☐ business
- ☐ discovery
- ☐
- ☐
- ☐

...in a way that will...

- ☐ provide
- ☐ transform
- ☐ ensure
- ☐
- ☐
- ☐

...

- ☐ the health / wealth of an entire continent.
- ☐ a fulfilling workplace for future generations.
- ☐ the way people age / drive / communicate.
- ☐

Write out your Personal Vision here:

My Personal Mission

The practical path I foresee taking (what I will physically do in the world) to realise my vision:

I will achieve my vision by

- ☐ working in a satisfying job until I retire on a good pension at 65.
- ☐ building a sustainable business that provides XYZ (specify) to ABC (specify).
- ☐ writing a book and promoting it through lectures around the world.
- ☐ developing an app that disrupts the XYZ (specify) industry.
- ☐ devoting myself to research and publication in my specialist field.
- ☐
- ☐
- ☐
- ☐

Write out your Mission statement here:

My Personal Motto

The motto that I choose to live by:

- ☐ "When life gives you lemons, make lemonade."
- ☐ "Always look on the bright side of life."
- ☐ "Everybody deserves a chance to express themselves without being criticised or judged."
- ☐

Write out your chosen Personal Motto here:

My Personal Daily Prayer

If I may ask anything of God / life / the Universe it would be:

- ☐ "Oh, Divine Providence, I ask not for more riches, but more wisdom with which to accept and use wisely the riches I received at birth in the form of the power to control and direct my mind to whatever ends I desire." —suggested by Napoleon Hill, author of *Think & Grow Rich*
- ☐

Write out your chosen Personal Daily Prayer here:

My Current Growth Themes

My current areas of growth are:

- ☐ Self-acceptance
- ☐ Being my word
- ☐
- ☐
- ☐

Write out your Current Growth Themes here:

My Checkpoints

Things I've learned that I wish to constantly be reminded of:

- ☐
- ☐
- ☐
- ☐
- ☐
- ☐

My Lifestyle Goals

The things I wish to have in my life, and by when. What I'll need to do, and who I'll need to be, in order to achieve them.

My Financial Goals

Have Eg. R10m in the bank, earning R1m a year interest, by end 2025.

Do Eg. Invest R10k a month in unit trusts.

Be Eg. Disciplined / Frugal

My Career Goals

Have Eg. CEO of an ethical, sustainable Fortune 500 company in the food industry by end 2025.

Do Eg. Identify and build networks. Work closely with HR to identify the steps and make sure I'm considered for the right promotions.

Be Eg. The most professionally competent and ethical leader I can be.

My Family Goals

Have Eg. Happy and harmonious home with children all in university and getting good grades. Weekly contact with all members. All together at least once a year/month.

Do Eg. Deal with fallout of divorce and get son out of rehab.

Be Eg. A parent who kids actually want to be with.

My Social Goals

Have Eg. Three close friends who are independent and whom I see once a month each on their own. Host one dinner party a year. Be invited to one dinner party a quarter.

Do Eg. Maintain regular contact, making one casual phone call a week.

Be Eg. The kind of friend I would want others to be to me.

My Spiritual Goals

Have Eg. A daily meditation and spiritual practice and prayer time that I adhere to.

Do Eg. Define the practice, learn what I need to learn (read / attend courses) and get up early in order to do it every day.

Be Eg. As dedicated as a monk.

My Physical Goals

Have Eg. Body Mass Index (BMI) <25; Percent Body Fat (PBF) <20%. Able to run 5km in under 30 mins and lift 60kg bench press.

Do Eg. Train at least 4 times a week. Research and define a diet and stick to it.

Be Eg. An obsessive gym freak who never misses a workout—except some-times.

My Leisure Goals

Have Eg. Visit one new country with spouse every year for at least 10 days. Or: Conduct one urban outing a month with spouse and friends.

Do Eg. Research, set aside funds, book early.

Be Eg. Interested and inquisitive.

My Intellectual Goals

Have Eg. A master's degree. Read 10 non-fiction books a year related to chosen field.

Do Eg. Research post-grad schools and register by end of current cycle. Allocate time in the diary for reading: two sessions a week of at least one hour each.

Be Eg. Clear about the value of this outcome and strict about setting boundaries and using the time.

NOTE Once you've completed this exercise, you may choose to write up the final version in a format that works for you and keep it in the place where you'll refer to it each day, perhaps your bedside table, in your dressing closet, in your briefcase or backpack, or in your top drawer at the office.

Template: Create My Day Checklist

SELECT ELEMENTS from the list below to create a reflection time at the beginning of each day, during which you will naturally refer to your
Legacy & Lifestyle Statement.

- ☐ Express gratitude for this life, for the day, the opportunities and for all that I have.

- ☐ Do some stretches or yoga poses to energise myself for the day (and put money in the health bank for when I get old).

- ☐ Meditate to practice being present and aware.

- ☐ Scan through my *Legacy & Lifestyle Statement* and focus on one element a day. Evaluate myself in terms of being my word and living out that element. Ask myself some coaching questions related to that aspect of the statement.

- ☐ Read through my *Checkpoints* list and reflect on what I've learned and decide where I can still apply that.

- ☐ Scan through my *Personal Effectiveness Handbook* and review one element a day. Commit to keep it present and top of mind all day.

- ☐ Define an empowering open question that I can ask myself throughout the day. (Or remind myself of my current open question, which I'm still busy with.)

- ☐ Define a performance or motivational state breakthrough for the week that I will promise myself to achieve. Optional: tell someone. (Or evaluate my progress towards the same.)

- ☐ Define one of my current goals as an "I am" statement (i.e. describe it as though it's already happening, as though I'm already living it) and write it down three times into my notebook or repeat it at least three times like a mantra during the day.

- ☐ Meditate to generate a positive feeling state towards the image of what has been expressed in my "I am…" statement.

- ☐ Review all my current commitments and make sure I'm on track.
- ☐ Deal with things I need to clear up (that I committed to do yesterday and did not do). Decide what to do, what to delegate, what to let go.
- ☐ Decide what I commit to doing today (and do it first thing, or as early as possible in the day).
- ☐ Commit to make any and all decisions that come up during the day as needing to be made.
- ☐ Commit to creating at least one new completion today.
- ☐ Surrender to my word / commit to do what I say I will do.
- ☐ Put myself in a receiving state and say, 'Thank you, I have received.'
- ☐
- ☐
- ☐
- ☐

NOTE Once you've decided which of these you'll do and how often—and perhaps added a few of your own—you may choose to write up the final list in a format that works for you and keep it in the place where you'll refer to it each day, perhaps your bedside table, in your dressing closet, in your briefcase or backpack, or in your top drawer at the office.

CHECK-OUT — DO THIS NOW

My Main Goal: Outcomes Assessment

REFER BACK to the objectives you set at the beginning of this book, then read and follow the instructions below.

For each of your main goals or objectives listed at the beginning of this program, reflect on what you have achieved. Score yourself as a percentage and record the relevant evidence and follow-up actions.

Main Goal	Measurable outcome	Level achieved	Evidence
A	Transfer the measurable outcome from your goals sheet to this space.	Self xx%	Provide evidence to support your self-assessment.

Forwarding Actions / Continuation

What actions could you think of that will support you to achieve the outcome 100% and/or to continue to grow in this area?

Main Goal	Measurable outcome	Level achieved	Evidence
B	Transfer the measurable outcome from your goals sheet to this space.	Self xx%	Provide evidence to support your self-assessment.

Forwarding Actions / Continuation

What actions could you think of that will support you to achieve the outcome 100% and/or to continue to grow in this area?

Main Goal	Measurable outcome	Level achieved	Evidence
C	Transfer the measurable outcome from your goals sheet to this space.	Self xx%	Provide evidence to support your self-assessment.

Forwarding Actions / Continuation

What actions could you think of that will support you to achieve the outcome 100% and/or to continue to grow in this area?

NOTE Once you've decided on your forwarding actions, you may choose to transfer them to your *Legacy & Lifestyle Statement* and/or your *Create My Day* worksheet, where you'll refer to them regularly. Or you may choose to post them up somewhere where you'll see them each day.

Epilogue | True Leadership

When you say, "I decided this or that…" you really believe that the "I" that is speaking is some kind of self-created entity, like you spoke yourself into being one day and then you decided who you would become.

Carl Jung said, "All modern people … assume that there is nothing … that they have not made up. We think we have invented everything physical – that nothing would be done if we did not do it; for that is our basic idea and it is an extraordinary assumption."

If you look more closely at the evidence that is available to you, you will see that you did not create yourself—your *self*—in this way. You found yourself having been born into a family and a country and a time that you did not ask for and every decision you made was a reaction to that.

An objective observation reveals that who you are—your *self*—emerged and took residence. You find yourself with it, making decisions that seek to further that same sense of self.

When we see this clearly, two possibilities open up.

Forgiveness happens as a natural consequence, and the possibility of true leadership emerges.

Firstly, the possibility that you can create yourself completely anew. You can decide to become someone who has no reference to your past. This does not mean you have to destroy your past or everything about it. There will certainly be many things you want to keep. However, it does create some freedom about what you can choose to do and who you can choose to be. You do not have to be *everything* which you have become.

Secondly, you see that, having assumed that you created yourself, you tend to treat other people as though they made themselves up too, as though they woke up one day and chose to be the way they are, with all their faults and shortcomings.

When you see that people did not choose who they have become, but rather find themselves being the way they are, this opens up the space for compassion and empathy. Forgiveness happens as a natural consequence, and the possibility of true leadership emerges, as you then seek to guide people towards seeing this for themselves, and creating new possibilities for their own lives.

BIBLIOGRAPHY

Barlow, David. *Clinical Handbook of Psychological Disorders: A Step-By-Step Treatment Manual*. New York: The Guilford Press, 2008.

Barlow, David et al. *Unified Protocol for Transdiagnostic Treatment of Emotional Disorders*. New York: Oxford University Press, 2011.

Beck, Aaron. *Cognitive Therapy and the Emotional Disorders*. New York: Meridian (Penguin), 1979.

Chatterjee, Debashis. *Leading Consciously*. Boston: Butterworth-Heinemann, 1998.

Csikszentmihalyi, Mihaly. *Flow: The Psychology of Happiness*. London: Rider (Penguin Random House), 2002.

Damasio, Antonio. *Descarte's Error*. New York: GP Putnam Sons, 1994.

Demartini, John. *The Values Factor*. New York: Berkley Books, 2013.

Gershon, Michael. *The Second Brain*. New York: Harper Collins, 1999.

Goleman, Daniel & Davidson, Richard J. *The Science of Meditation*. London: Penguin Life (Penguin Random House), 2017.

Halbfass, Wilhelm. *On Being and What There Is*. Delhi: Sri Satguru Publications, 1992.

Herbert, Wray. *To Thine Own Self: The Psychology of Authenticity*. https://www.psychologicalscience.org/news/were-only-human/to-thine-own-self-the-psychology-of-authenticity.html, 23 January 2015.

Hollis, James. *Swamplands of the Soul*. Toronto: Inner City Books, 1996.

Horney, Karen. *Our Inner Conflicts*. Oxford: Routledge, 1946 (Digital Version, 2007).

Horney, Karen. *Neurosis and Human Growth*. Oxford: Routledge, 1951 (Digital Version, 2007).

Jung, Carl (Ed.). *Man and His Symbols*. London: Picador, 1978.

Kotler, Steven. *The Science of Peak Human Performance*. http://time.com/56809/the-science-of-peak-human-performance/, 30 April 2014.

Krishnamurti, Jiddu. *Facing A World in Crisis*. Cape Town: Spearhead, 2005.

LeDoux, Joseph. *The Emotional Brain*. New York: Touchstone (Simon & Schuster), 1998.

Lehrhaupt, Linda & Meibert, Petra. *Mindfulness-Based Stress Reduction*. Novato, California: New World Library, 2017.

Lehrer, Jonathan. *How We Decide*. Boston: Houghton Mifflin Harcourt, 2009.

Lehrer, Paul M., Woolfolk, Robert L. & Sime, Wesley E. *Principles and Practice of Stress Management (3rd Ed)*. New York: The Guilford Press, 2007.

Linde, Colinda. *A Cognitive-Relaxation-Visualisation Intervention for Anxiety in Cancer Patients*. Rand Afrikaans University (University of Johannesburg), 2000.

McGonigal, Kelly. *The Upside of Stress*. New York: Avery (Penguin Random House), 2016.

McTaggart, John. *The Theme of Transcendence in Georg Simmel's Social Theory*. McMaster University. http://hdl.handle.net/11375/15572, September 1989.

Robbins, Tony. *Awaken the Giant Within*. New York: Simon & Schuster, 1992.

Ruiz, Miguel. *The Four Agreements*. San Rafael, California: Amber-Allen Publishing, 1997.

Ruiz, Miguel. *The Voice of Knowledge*. San Rafael, California: Amber-Allen Publishing, 2004.

Segal, Zindel, Williams, Mark & Teasdale, John. *Mindfulness-Based Cognitive Therapy for Depression: A New Approach to Preventing Relapse*. New York: The Guilford Press, 2002.

Selye, Hans. *Stress and Disease*. Science (122, 625-631), 1955.

Selye, Hans. *Confusion and Controversy in the Stress Field*. Journal of Human Stress (1, 37-44), 1975.

Senge, Peter. *The Fifth Discipline: The Art and Practice of the Learning Organization (Second Edition)*. New York: Doubleday/Currency, 2002.

Singer, Michael. *The Surrender Experiment*. New York: Harmony Books, 2015.

Singer, Michael. *The Untethered Soul*. Oakland, California: New Harbinger Publications, 2007.

Tirch, Dennis, Silberstein, Laura R. & Kolts, Russell L. *Buddhist Psychology and Cognitive-Behaviour Therapy: A Clinician's Guide*. New York: The Guilford Press, 2016.

Tolle, Eckhart. *A New Earth*. London: Penguin Books, 2005.

Yates, John & Immergut, Matthew. *The Mind Illuminated*. New York: Touchstone, 2017.

FURTHER RESOURCES

Coaching

Neil offers various coaching options, including Life Coaching, Coaching for Men, Executive Coaching and Team Coaching. These can be delivered in person or via videocall. There are also online self-coaching options available.

www.neilbierbaum.com

The Man Matrix

The Man Matrix is a website dedicated to helping men understand themselves, and women understand men. Discover the two axes of men's personality and development. Identity where you fit in and draw your own free or paid personal report.

www.themanmatrix.com

Practical Mindfulness

The *Practical Mindfulness* program is conducted live in Johannesburg, South Africa and, by invitation, in cities around the world. There is also an online self-study version, which can be branded and packaged for corporate clients, as well as a book, in printed and e-book versions.

www.practicalmindfulness.co.za.

Self-Help CBT

Thoughtsfirst is a self-help CBT website with a range of resources for people suffering from anxiety and worry, stress, social phobia, insomnia and panic attacks.

www.thoughtsfirst.com